JESUS
CALLED HER
MOTHER

JESUS CALLED HER MOTHER

DEE JEPSEN

BETHANY HOUSE PUBLISHERS
MINNEAPOLIS, MINNESOTA 55438

Published by Bethany House Publishers
A Ministry of Bethany Fellowship, Inc.
6820 Auto Club Road, Minneapolis, Minnesota 55438

Printed in the United States of America

Library of Congress Cataloging-in-Publication Data

Jepsen, Dee.
    Jesus called her mother / Dee Jepsen.
        p.   cm.

    1. Mary, Blessed Virgin, Saint—Theology.   I. Title.
BT613.J47   1992
232.91—dc20   92–31393
ISBN 1–55661–295–8   CIP

I dedicate this book to all God's women
who seek to serve Him with all their
hearts in the fullness of their womanhood.

DEE JEPSEN is presently the national campaign director for the "Enough Is Enough" campaign, which mobilizes women to combat pornography's exploitation of children. The wife of the former U.S. Senator Roger Jepsen, she has served as a special assistant to the President as well as many other national positions. An award-winning writer, she is the author of *Women: Beyond Equal Rights*, *What's Happening in My World*, and *Women: The Challenge and the Call*. The Jepsens make their home in the Washington, D.C. area and have six grown children.

Contents

Introduction · 11

1 / The Mother Jesus Loved · 17

2 / A Willing Heart · 33

3 / Celebrating Truth: Woman to Woman · 47

4 / A Son Is Given · 63

5 / Counting the Cost · 79

6 / Courage for the Call · 93

7 / Learning to Let Go · 109

8 / "Whatever He Tells You—Do It" · 123

9 / Our True Family · 139

10 / The Sword Pierces · 153

11 / Sent · 167

12 / A Model of True Womanhood · 181

Introduction

The event of Christ's birth through a woman says volumes to me about the worth of women and the importance of motherhood. Yet today, women struggle with their identity, with their roles, choices, rights, and responsibilities. Even Christian women often have perplexing questions: How can I know what God wants me to do with my life? How can I be sure of hearing His call, answering it faithfully, and fulfilling it?

How ironic, in this age when every woman seems to seek a role model, that many of us tend to overlook one of the most inspiring examples of fulfilled womanhood the Bible offers: Mary of Nazareth. God chose Mary, among all possible women, to give birth to His Son. It's true that Mary has been overly idealized by some, but she has also become a mere shadow to others. I have found in Scripture the evidence of her touch, the imprint of her obedient steps. Mary lived a different lifestyle in a different age, but her character qualities shine—and more than that, they can be applied to contemporary life because they are eternal attributes that never become outdated.

Personally, I find it unfortunate that Mary continues to be a point of division among believers. Some of this is based on misunderstanding, and some on genuine doctrinal disagreement. I believe it need not be so. Certainly some doctrines rise above dispute: Jesus Christ is God's Son; He is our Savior, who died to pay for our sins; He rose from the dead and sits at the Father's right hand; and our salvation comes only through believing in and accepting Him. These beliefs are essential to all authentic streams of Christianity.

Beyond these core doctrines are gray areas of varying opinion. Must Christians enjoy uniformity of all doctrine to find unity in His Spirit? Must all Christian women share an identical understanding of Mary's place in theology in order to appreciate her, learn from her, or value and emulate the traits she possessed? I believe not.

I grew up in a Catholic home. In those early days I believed in God and prayed to Him, though He seemed so distant I wasn't quite sure He heard. I was certainly aware of Mary and the devotion many reserved for her. Yet I had no particular feelings about Mary one way or the other. I felt no special sense of devotion, nor have I felt a need to reject or resent her.

Since that time, my faith has deepened into a personal, daily walk with the Lord. He is not distant anymore, because I answered His invitation to draw near in faith. It's a standing invitation to each person, and answering it with a yes is to me the single most important decision any woman or man can make. And beyond that single decision, we are left to seek God daily, to find His plan and pattern for our lives. Sometimes that pattern only begins to reveal itself as we look back and reflect, combing our way through difficult and joyous events until we see a coherent picture emerge.

Like so many women, I can only marvel at God's constant grace through struggles that seemed overwhelming and confusing at times. I grew up as a farm girl, left motherless at thirteen. After going through a divorce when I felt I had no other choice (even though I did not believe in divorce), I struggled as a single parent. I have been a homemaker, co-founder of a small business, and the wife of a politician. By God's grace, all these "bits" have united into a meaningful whole; through daily prayer, I have come to understand God's plan for my life and to appreciate the fact that He has a plan for every one of us. And I have come to see that contemporary women are hungering for mentors: examples of integrated womanhood at its finest. One constant that has emerged in my life is the need to encourage my sisters to reach for the spiritual goals God has for them. And so I write this book for all who honestly seek examples and inspiration from the lives of women who have come before us.

I have focused my attention often on Mary because she lived a life that was pleasing to God. For that reason she belongs to all of us—that is, to all who believe in her son Jesus. In researching beliefs and attitudes about Mary, I conferred with David du Plessis, known as "Mr. Pentecost." For many years before he died, David felt a need to reach out in love to Roman Catholics. Being a Pentecostal preacher, he endured much criticism for this mission. Yet David opened a dialogue that continues to bring understanding between many Catholics and Protestants. His view of Mary shaped my own: "Catholics have adored Mary and Protestants have ignored her. Neither is right."

This writing is not slanted toward any particular doctrinal view of Mary. I have attempted to acknowledge legitimate denominational differences in these chapters, but those differences are not my focus. Instead, I sense a distinct call to present what I have learned from the life of one young Jewish girl who found favor with God, so much

13

so that she became the mother of His Son.

And in the writing, I have grown in the conviction that it is time for all who believe in Jesus to consider His mother again. Although Mary's call was distinctive, her life speaks to all women today. She was blessed *among* women—she was not lifted *above* us. She offers a premier model of how a woman may receive God's call in her life, respond to the call, rejoice in it, and remain faithful to it, no matter what.

Join me in getting reacquainted with a woman whose life example can bring new focus and vision to your life.

In the sixth month, God sent the angel Gabriel to Nazareth, a town in Galilee, to a virgin pledged to be married to a man named Joseph, a descendant of David. The virgin's name was Mary.

LUKE 1:26–27

1

The Mother Jesus Loved

SOMETIMES IN THE MIDST of the very ordinary, the God of the universe visits us in an extraordinary way. Mary, the mother of Jesus, experienced such a visit when the angel Gabriel appeared to her, announcing news of the baby she would bear. Reading the Bible, we can wonder why such powerful events took place in bygone days. Were young women more pious then? Less busy? More favored by God? Is there something about Mary and others like her that we need to rediscover for ourselves?

God is no less active now than in Mary's day. He still makes His presence known to believers in ways that are unmistakable. His Spirit still quietly but surely speaks and leads us to walk in His plan.

To begin, I should explain how I've learned to hear His

strong, sure, "still small voice," even in ordinary events. . . .

On a May morning in Virginia's Shenandoah Mountains, my spirit was soaring with the freshness of spring among the green hills. This would be a relaxing day spent savoring a favorite place: "Canaan," our farm retreat in the Blue Ridge Mountains.

I wandered down to the clear, still lake next to our fields and pushed against the dock to launch our paddle boat. The forest and water were waking from their winter hibernation, and the air was scented with promise. Flowers pushed from their buds; bright green grass was smooth as untrampled new carpet.

Slowly I worked the boat's pedals, propelling my little craft quietly across the mirroring water, expecting nothing more than a bit of healthy exercise and fresh air. *How peaceful!* Gliding gently to the far side of the lake, I began to sing a song of praise to the Lord for the goodness of life. He had blessed me with a redeemed life and marriage, with six grown children, and now with grandchildren. It was a restful moment in the midst of our usually hectic life, which includes a pressing travel and organizational schedule. I was about to begin another round of speaking engagements and was sorely in need of quiet reflection. Was there something new and inspiring I could say to the many, many women I was going to address in the upcoming months?

And then, clearly and gently, a word came, interrupting my thoughts: *Mary.*

The Bible says that God speaks in "a still small voice" (1 Kings 19:12, KJV). Usually He speaks through the Scriptures, other people, circumstances, and our consciences. But sometimes He speaks to our hearts through a compelling inward impression. That is how I experienced His presence there on the lake.

In that silent moment, His presence was as real as it sometimes is in the hushed solitude of a cathedral. Tears filled my eyes, and my mind raced back through years—through centuries—to the hills and plains of Israel.

When Jesus walked this earth, He was both God and man. The Bible says He was subject to all the temptations common to us. *And,* I thought, *He was subject to every human emotion as well.* He was angry at the harsh legalists. He laughed with His friends. Sorrow for the pain of hurting people moved Him to act with compassion. He felt love for His own mother. . . . As God, Jesus would have loved Mary the same way He loves all of us. But as man, He loved her as His mother. This was a new thought for me.

What was that like—to be loved as Jesus' mother? No other human has ever received an honor like Mary's: The Father chose to send His only Son into the world through her. And Mary was the only human privileged to be present at both Jesus' birth *and* death. According to tradition, Mary's husband, Joseph, died sometime before the crucifixion, and he is not mentioned after Jesus' visit to the temple as a boy.

I was suddenly intrigued by this quiet figure—Mary—who patiently followed in Jesus' steps. Mary not only experienced firsthand the birth and death of Jesus, she also saw Jesus soon after the Resurrection and was present at His Ascension. She remained faithful to Him, even when His most devoted disciples fled out of fear and confusion. Quite likely she was also present at Pentecost, when God sent the Holy Spirit to indwell and empower believers.

I was moved, too, to realize how Jesus had shown

loyalty and love toward His mother even in His darkest hour. As He hung on the cross, suspended in agony between life and death, His mother's comfort and security were not forgotten. He must have spoken with extreme difficulty, nailed to that wicked instrument of death, saying to Mary, "Dear woman, here is your son," and to John, "Here is your mother" (John 19:26–27). And so, He gave His mother into John's care. These, some of His last words from the cross, arose out of compassion for her.

I continued to drift on the lake, reflecting that, although Mary is rarely mentioned in biblical accounts, the moments when she *is* mentioned, she seems to be acting in the center of God's will. True, she wasn't flamboyant, jumping out of a boat to walk on water, like Peter. She didn't need heavenly lightning in order for God to get her attention, like Paul. She simply remained available to do what God wanted with her life. Walking quietly and courageously in His plan, she was obedient and faithful.

But what does Mary have to do with me? I wondered as I paddled to shore and docked my boat. *Or other women of today?*

After that day, I began searching the Scriptures, examining references to Mary and trying to understand her life and character. It seemed to me there was significance in the timing of my studies: In a few days, I would fly to California to speak to a large church on Mother's Day.

As I prepared for my talk, I spent time in prayer pondering the Crucifixion—imagining it from Mary's perspective. I sensed a small measure of the emotional pain Mary felt as she watched her son die. Jesus was innocent—sinless—yet they condemned Him. They mocked and insulted Him, spit on Him, and stripped off His clothing. How deeply it must have hurt this woman, who was so powerless to stop the machinery of politics and the forces of evil from hurting her grown child.

As I sensed Mary's grief, an image arose in my heart: Jesus had looked down from the cross and seen His mother watching Him die. Was He tempted to spare His mother pain, as an earthly son might be? Because of His love for all of us, He allowed her heart to be broken.

There is no greater sacrifice, no gift more important, than Jesus' death for us. But I cannot comprehend God's love with my finite mind. I *can*, however, understand the love between a mother and child. I found myself growing to appreciate Mary in a new way. And during my trip to California, I did something unusual for a Protestant speaking to a Protestant audience on Mother's Day: I dwelled on Mary the mother of Jesus as an example for all mothers.

From then, I felt as if I were being nudged to continue learning about this unique woman. Roger was still a U.S. Senator at the time, and one Sunday morning we were in Paris, returning home from a diplomatic trip. We had awakened early and decided to find a church, so we climbed into a taxi. The driver wound his way up a steep hillside, where I caught sight of the Cathedral of *Sacre Coeur*. High above Paris, it seemed to stand like a watchful angel, guarding the city.

We entered into the stone-coolness, hearing the hushed tones of morning mass being celebrated in the center of the magnificent sanctuary, which was cordoned off by a velvet rope. I felt warmed and welcomed by the scent of burning candles, the aroma of frankincense, and the brilliant hues of stained-glass windows all around. Roger stopped to study the windows and I, lost in thought, wandered alone toward the front section of the church. Something high above caught my eye.

21

An enormous mosaic had been created up over the altar. I gazed at the scene made of thousands of tiny colored ceramic pieces fitted together. As the mosaic caught the morning sun, it was alight with shades of red, blue, green, and white. It was a depiction of heaven, and I noticed a woman worshiping Jesus, who stood in the center of it all. The woman was Mary.

Again, just as had happened on the lake a month earlier, an inner impression came. Mary had run her own race of faith and finished the course—she had surely met a welcome of honor when she entered the courts of heaven. All of life's sorrow and upheaval are behind her now. She stands worshiping Jesus as He rules in glory. As in this lovely picture, so it must be in spirit: Her entire demeanor directs onlookers not toward her but toward her son.

I reflected on the mosaic, too, as a work of art: A mosaic's theme makes sense when it is viewed from a distant perspective. Seeing it up close detracts from the overall picture because the individual bits of tile stand out. *That's just how it is with every woman's life*, I thought. *So often, I become focused only on the scattered fragments of my busy days and lose sight of the whole—the image of God's plan for my life.*

How do I keep my focus on the Lord—on His patterns and purposes? I mused. It was the sort of question I'd been addressing in recent years, not only for myself, but also for thousands of women I'd spoken to.

That day in *Sacre Coeur* was nearly twenty years after I'd committed my life to Jesus Christ. For six of those years, Roger had been serving in the U.S. Senate. I had worked at the White House as a liaison between President Reagan and women's organizations, had served on my husband's staff, and had helped with his campaign. I'd found myself in the front line of issues confronting women: abortion, equal rights, child-care, pornography. I'd seen firsthand the disruptive and misleading tactics used by some of the more militant feminist organizations intent on their particular agendas. And I'd witnessed the confusion and anxiety experienced by so many ordinary women who feel like failures because they do not measure up to society's definitions of success and achievement. Through it all, I'd grown to have a deep concern for the inner needs of contemporary women, whatever their background, role, or calling. The desire to focus them on God's purposes was now one of the patterns that had emerged in my own life.

I attempted in the White House, for example, to promote healing, not hostility. Many of the concerns raised by responsible women activists were valid: Most women have, at some time in their lives, been treated unjustly; and most have faced a double standard or a lack of respect. There are certainly reasons to desire change. But I'd become convinced of an urgent need for something more— something beyond angry protests, new laws, and more demands. What women need most, I came to see, is to come to terms with their identity as individuals created in the image of God.

That conviction in no way diminished with time. After leaving the White House, I wrote about my experiences as a liaison to women's groups. *Women: Beyond Equal Rights* expressed my desire for women to find personhood and peace—two elements that can help us see past the fragments of our hectic lives and focus instead on the purposes God had in mind when He made us. As I spoke to women after the book's publication, I kept hearing the same questions: What does it mean to be a woman of godly character? Do the Bible's directives really apply to me today? How can I know whether I'm making the right choices about what to do with my life? Everywhere, women were looking for heroines, mentors, role models.

Gazing at Mary's focused expression there at *Sacre Coeur*, I thought, *Perhaps this woman has something to teach me—and to teach other women—about responding to the challenges God calls us to face.*

Timeless Traits

Mary indeed stands out among New Testament figures as the one person who knew the most about Jesus; who knew Him from boyhood and understood His humanity more thoroughly than anyone else. Yet the mosaic of Mary that emerges from the New Testament is just that, a portrait made of tiny fragments. If we want to learn who Mary was, we have our work cut out for us.

The task is well worth pursuing, though. From my efforts, I've concluded that Mary was just the sort of woman I'd like to be. Ultimately, she emerged as a model of apparently unflagging faithfulness. Where did she learn the secret of her godliness—the humility that allowed her to make herself available to do what God wanted?

Other questions come to mind as well, starting from the moment the angel Gabriel made his stunning announcement: What caused Mary to respond immediately by praising God and trusting Him, even though it meant a great personal risk? Did she know from the outset that saying yes to God would bring personal hardship and turmoil? What did she gain by seeking the fellowship of other godly women, especially her cousin Elizabeth? How had she come to be so familiar with the Word of God and so faithful in training her son? As a mother, what sort of characteristics did Mary display? How does her life speak to mothers today who face so many challenges—mothers who yearn for characteristics such as physical stamina, empathy, rapport, perseverance, courage, and emotional resilience? Each of these questions will be examined in the chapters that follow, and I believe the answers can enrich the life of every woman today.

Undergirding all of Mary's traits is one crucial attitude, which she displayed when Gabriel told her she would bear the Son of God. Mary naturally wondered how she could have a child, since she was still a virgin—to which Gabriel replied, "Nothing is impossible with God."

Mary's immediate response shows her attitude: "I am the Lord's servant. May it be to me as you have said" (Luke 1:38, NIV). In all the circumstances that followed, even when life seemed thoroughly impossible, Mary would offer that same spirit of trust.

"Nothing is impossible with God."

"May it be to me as you have said."

I believe this brief dialogue holds the most important attitude—the "heart posture"—toward God and His promises that many of us need to rediscover in this age of individual rights. It requires a willing acceptance of God's truth in our lives, *no matter what the circumstances.* Our human nature can leave us warring within. Sometimes we forget God's power and presence and tend to despair. We buy into the lie that our choices don't really matter anyway. Or we lean toward a prideful attitude—one that says, "Nothing is impossible for *me.*" We grasp at power and position, believing we can take charge of our lives and our circumstances.

Today, we are in the midst of a war to win over the hearts of women. The issues have gone far deeper than "equal rights." Today, women demand financial and even reproductive autonomy from men. They want *in*dependence rather than healthy *inter*dependence. In this struggle, women are patterning themselves after another woman— one that most women, frankly, hate to be reminded of: Eve.

The Other "Model"

Eve sought to be like God—to possess for herself the "knowledge of good and evil." She was deceived into disobeying God's explicit command.

Commentators have noted the stark contrast between Mary and Eve. Charles Spurgeon, a giant of the Christian faith in the last century, notes, "Since venturous woman led the way in the sin that brought forth Paradise Lost, she, and she alone, ushers in the Regainer of Paradise."[1] Mary was content to be herself—and to let God be God. God had much in store for her, and she was willing to receive it in His time, never knowing exactly what lay ahead.

In 1 Corinthians, Paul draws a line of comparison between Adam and Jesus: "As in Adam all die, so in Christ all will be made alive (15:22). His observation invites further comparison of Eve with Mary. The serpent came to Eve; an angel was sent from God to Mary. There was a moment in time when both Eve and Mary had to choose to obey or disobey God. Eve made the decision to say no to God, which brought condemnation to humankind; Mary made the decision to say yes to God, which brought salvation to mankind. Eve said in essence, "I will be like God." Mary said, "God's will be done." And because she placed her will fully in God's hands, total redemption came to us through Mary's son.

Notice this: It was only after Mary's choice had been made, her commitment affirmed, that God's full plan for her life began to appear. At every step of the way, as we will see, Mary had to confront similar choices, moments in which she could choose to say yes or no to God.

The search for a true picture of Mary, then, will also be a search through those areas of *our* lives that have yet to reply yes to the Creator.

Mary, Our Mentor

Ultimately my search for a deeper, broader picture of Mary has convinced me that this woman belongs to us all—that is, to all who believe in her son, Jesus. In our Protestant churches, we base sermons on the lives of Peter and Paul and various disciples, as well as prophets and other Old Testament figures. Why are Protestant sermons about the life of Mary nearly nonexistent, when her life *is* a sermon?

Recently, *Time* magazine reported, "Both the adoration and the conflict attending Mary have risen to extraordinary levels. A grass-roots revival of faith in the Virgin is taking place worldwide."[2] Record numbers of people are visiting churches and chapels built to commemorate her. At the same time, Catholic scholars and activists are debating Mary's image, calling into question her traditional portrayal by their own church.

Throughout the church's early centuries, Mary was regarded as the "mother of God" by all believers. This title was given to her not to elevate her, but to emphasize the truth that Jesus Christ was *truly God* and *truly man,* a doctrine under attack. A leading evangelical scholar, Kenneth Kantzer, comments on the practice of calling Mary the mother of God: "While the phrase may be awkward, Protestants generally have agreed that it is faithful to the real sense of Scripture, and that to deny it is to suggest that we really do not believe in the full deity of Him who was born of Mary."[3]

Later, the Roman Catholic Church added to this concept by adopting doctrines regarding Mary that are not based on Scripture. The main Catholic doctrines concerning Mary are: She remained a virgin throughout her life; she was conceived without original sin (known to Catholics as the Immaculate Conception); she participated with Jesus in redeeming mankind; and she was miraculously taken into heaven (the Assumption).

Protestants reject these beliefs because they are not found in the Bible and because they appear to elevate Mary to a spiritual position equal to or exceeding the position Jesus holds. Reacting against such doctrines, Protestants have gone to great lengths to ignore Mary entirely. Poet Luci Shaw points out:

> At Christmas, most Protestants are tolerant enough to allow Mary limited access onto our greeting cards and into our creches and carols. But the rest of the year she is a victim of simple neglect. In bending over backward to avoid certain excesses of veneration, we have abandoned Mary to a kind of evangelical limbo.[4]

Perhaps there is a place in the middle—a patch of common ground—where a down-to-earth, biblically based portrait of Mary might speak to us all. That is my fervent hope and prayer for this book. I pray it will serve as a vehicle for helping today's women of all persuasions to learn from this woman of old. And I pray that her experiences and her example will promote unity of spirit, not division, in spite of genuine differences in the practice of our faith. For Mary points us to Jesus.

There is, despite our variances, at least one thing almost all believers agree on: the rare beauty and clear prophetic message of Mary's *Magnificat*—that song of praise that burst from deep within when she visited her cousin Elizabeth. Mary said, "From now on all generations will call me *blessed*" (Luke 1:48).

Just what does it mean to be "blessed"? How can we understand this concept in order to see how it applies to Mary and what that means to us? Do we know enough about Mary to understand why she was blessed? Do we recognize in her the traits God favors? Or have we ignored Mary and the lessons of her life to our own detriment?

As I began to contemplate the life of Mary, I developed a hunger to know more about her, to make her more than a cold, tile mosaic—an image made up of fragments I could not yet piece together for myself. So I embarked on months of reading and studying about Mary, and I traveled to Israel in search of answers. I wanted to walk where Mary had walked and lived, to get in touch with her land and life.

What I found in Israel and elsewhere left me more convinced than ever that Mary consistently charted a path sought desperately by so many women today: a way of life that caused her to hear God's call, understand it, and respond to it faithfully. I could not help but allow my imagination to fill in details of her thoughts and feelings, knowing as I did that I was looking back, limited by my own time, culture, and views. I hope readers will overlook when necessary my own interpretations of Mary, and be helped by those views that inspire.

I invite you to walk the pathway of Mary's life now,

as I have. Let her choices challenge you or confirm you in your own. I guarantee you will come closer to understanding God's plan and pattern for your life in this age when God is searching for women of strength and character.

The angel went to [Mary] and said, "Greetings, you who are highly favored! The Lord is with you."

Mary was greatly troubled at his words and wondered what kind of greeting this might be. But the angel said to her, "Do not be afraid, Mary, you have found favor with God. You will be with child and give birth to a son, and you are to give him the name Jesus. He will be great and will be called the Son of the Most High. . . .

"How will this be," Mary asked the angel, "since I am a virgin?"

The angel answered, "The Holy Spirit will come upon you, and the power of the Most High will overshadow you. . . . For nothing is impossible with God."

"I am the Lord's servant," Mary answered. "May it be to me as you have said." Then the angel left her.

LUKE 1:28–38

2

A Willing Heart

ON A HOT SUMMER AFTERNOON, I stood within a few feet of the spot where tradition says heaven encountered earth nearly two thousand years ago. A young Hebrew girl met the angel Gabriel, whose name means "Mighty One of God," and who bore the mightiest message ever sent to humankind. Like lightning out of darkness, he came to tell of a promised event that would change the lives of untold millions for time and eternity.

Here lies the wonder: God reveals the mystery of His incarnation—His salvation plan—to a poor, unknown teenage girl in an obscure location, the hill town of Nazareth. The highest messenger with the highest message came to Galilee, considered Israel's most backward region, to the town of Nazareth, which was the least of the Galilean cities. In Jesus' time, Nathanael asked incredulously,

"Can anything good come from there?" (John 1:46).

As a contemporary tourist, I was surprised at the disdain many Israelis still hold toward Nazareth, now a poverty-stricken Arab village. My daughter and I had set out from the port city of Haifa in a rented car. Along a highway lined with orange groves and olive orchards, we stopped to ask directions from a middle-aged gentleman, who began gesturing widely in true Middle-Eastern fashion. He pointed out the appropriate turn, then he looked at me with great puzzlement. "Lady, why do you want to go to Nazareth?"

My mental response was, *I'm searching for Mary—trying to discover who she was.* But after about a week it had occurred to me, *Although I'm looking for Mary, I keep finding Jesus.*

Somehow it seemed that was exactly how she would want it. The Lord might give us pearl after pearl regarding this woman who was "blessed among women," but they must always bring us to the "pearl of great price"—Jesus himself.

Where Mary Dwelled

On our way to Nazareth, my daughter and I drove through lowland stretches of road, where scrub trees and gnarled olives endure unrelenting sun. Putty-colored stones dot the landscape, and nomads dressed in white trek ever so slowly across the horizon. When Jesus called Nazareth "home," the surrounding terrain may have been somewhat greener with vegetation. Yet even if Nazareth was more fertile in those days, its reputation was dismal.

Nazareth lies to the north and west of the Sea of Galilee, rising from a narrow and secluded valley up a steep slope.

The encircling hills confine the view from the lower part of the city, but offer a wide range of vision from the summits. It is a rough-and-tumble village, with hilly streets and sidewalks littered with refuse. Small shops line the winding roads, and vendors holler at tourists, pressing them to buy their goods. The needle-like minarets of Muslim shrines surround the Christian Basilica of the Annunciation. Today, Nazareth is home to about 3,000 inhabitants, mostly day-laborers, but in the days of Jesus it was more of a small town than a city. It played host to the rough, worldly caravan merchants who traveled "the great road of commerce" that cut from the Jordan River through Galilee and across to the Mediterranean Sea coast.[1]

During the height of Jesus' ministry, Capernaum, which rests beside the Sea of Galilee, was known as His home. But throughout His ministry—and even after His ascension when He appeared to Saul of Tarsus—Jesus referred to himself as "Jesus of Nazareth." And so He chose to identify himself with His mother's hometown.

At the time that Gabriel appeared with his message, Mary was no more than a teenager, perhaps as young as fourteen. Like other Jewish girls her age, she most likely would have received no formal schooling. Instead, her days would have been spent helping her mother with essential household chores such as baking barley bread, hauling water from the village wells, spinning flax into cloth, mending clothes, and tending babies.

The only New Testament account of the angel's announcement appears in Luke's gospel. Luke, who was a Gentile physician and friend of the apostle Paul, was not present at the events he recorded about Jesus' life, and certainly was not present at the angel's announcement of Jesus' birth. Many scholars believe he got detailed information directly from Mary.

What was it like for Mary, in the midst of her mundane duties, to encounter a heavenly messenger? What would it be like for any one of us? The immediate significance of the event for Mary's life was astonishing. Until that moment, God had allowed only glimpses of His plan, revealed through prophetic words—but it had been nearly four hundred years since His chosen people had heard a whisper from God.

There is no way for us to know exactly how Mary responded to Gabriel's life-changing visit. Yet her biblical portrait is sketched in by faith and obedience. Keeping those two principles in mind, I found myself exploring the streets of Nazareth—and exploring with my imagination the emotions that an awestruck Mary may have experienced when the flaming messenger left God's word burning in her soul.

"Why Me, Lord?"

The messenger in the shining raiment vanished swiftly, like a candle's flame extinguished in a sudden gust of wind. Mary was alone.

She rubbed her eyes, dazzled, holding her breath. Could this really have happened? The angel had dwarfed her by his presence. He called himself Gabriel, and Mary had dropped to her knees, startled and frightened. He reassured her, and her fear changed to awe. And then, having delivered a message from God, the angel was gone, leaving her tingling with wonder.

Mary's heart beat rapidly, and her hands trembled. What did it mean? Would anyone believe her? Her own mother? Joseph?

She knelt motionless for a long time. Tears came spilling down her cheeks.

The pottery pitcher she was holding before the divine interruption sat empty before her, forgotten. How could she think of something so mundane as drawing water when words of such magnitude were flowing through her heart?

What do you do when heaven departs and only colorless stone walls remain? How do you explain it to others when the brilliance of heavenly light vanishes with its bearer, leaving only dust motes floating in sunlight that are dim by comparison?

Questions must have consumed her thoughts. *How could this be? How is it possible that I have found favor with God?* As a member of a tribal nation, she would have understood that the message was not for her alone, but for all of her people.

Her thoughts must have skimmed back over events that gave form and meaning to the lives of the people of Israel. Angelic visitors met with her forefathers—Abraham, Jacob, and many others.

She must remember the message exactly. *He said I was highly favored by God, and that I would bear a son who will reign as a king forever.* But did the holy prophets have anything to say about Nazareth? Mary reviewed the words of Isaiah, which she knew by heart from keeping the Sabbath and observing holy days. *The Messiah is to come through a virgin. I am a virgin. The prophet told us long ago, "Therefore the Lord shall give you a sign: Behold, a virgin shall conceive, and bear a son, and shall call his name Immanuel." Our people have prayed every day for the Messiah . . . but God has been silent so long.*

Perhaps Mary unconsciously ran her hands over the rough-woven fabric of the blue gown worn by virgin girls like herself. Taking the loose bottom edge of her sleeve, she wiped her tears, considering what this would mean in her own life. Her virginity was her first thought when Gabriel delivered his message about the child she would bear. She was betrothed to Joseph. He and her father had written a _Shetre Erusin_, a legal document of betrothal that could not be dissolved except by divorce. A breach of faithfulness would be regarded as adultery. Their marriage would not be consummated until after the wedding ceremony. As was the custom, the wedding festivities had been planned to run the course of an entire week.[2]

What about Joseph? Did the implications of her situation dawn on her? Would she lose the husband who was pledged to her? Others had made plans for her, but she had said yes to God's plan.

Then, of course, there were the villagers. _People will talk,_ she thought. Even if she could make her family understand, most people would assume she'd committed adultery. The punishment for women who were pregnant outside of marriage was death by stoning.[3] Although this law wasn't enforced in all of Israel, in Galilee it was considered adultery if a betrothed woman did not remain pure until after the actual wedding ceremony, the _nissu'in._

Still, she had spoken her commitment, her betrothal, to another. Was the angel even now standing before the wondrous throne with Mary's reply to God's message: _"Be it unto me . . ."_? Her thoughts began to shift. Through the years, God had shown He was "the God of the womb," moving miraculously for Sarah, Rachel, Hannah, and others. He had done the seemingly impossible: He had answered the prayers of barren women longing for children, and those women had become pregnant in spite of their advancing age. The angel had told her that her cousin Elizabeth was with child, though she had been barren and was too old to conceive.

But how would Mary conceive *this* baby? *"The Holy Spirit will come upon you . . . and overshadow you."*

Will I know when it happens? Is His life already starting to form within me? She must have pondered God's mysterious ways. When and how should she tell her mother?

No, being "highly favored" did not guarantee an easy life. Her people—God's chosen people—had suffered a great deal. The price for God's favor could be high indeed.

On that summer day in Nazareth, My daughter and I left the eye-dazzling brilliance of the Mediterranean noon behind and entered the cool interior of the Basilica. It took a moment for our eyes to adjust—to see the ancient stone dwelling, housed within the church itself. Centuries of tradition identify it as Mary's home. And it took another minute to see past the tourists and worshipers—to imagine Mary, in her room, rising to her feet and choosing a new destiny.

Drawing herself to her full height, and with a determination like the giants of faith who had preceded her, Mary declared for the ears of eternity, "So be it, my Lord. I believe you and I trust you."

What the days ahead would bring she could not guess. But she would step into God's plan for her life, whatever it would mean.

Saying Yes to God

Gabriel's visit caught Mary by surprise, but it did not catch her unprepared. God, who knew Mary's heart, also knew He had given her a free will. I wonder if the hosts of heaven waited, listening intently, as Mary made her decision.

It is the same for each of us; God prepares us, but we

hold the power to say yes or no to Him—to control our own lives or to give the control over to Him.

It was Mary's willing heart that changed everything. Eternity waited. Heaven listened. Our salvation hung in the balance. And then this one woman said, "Yes! I want what you want, God."

Mary displayed several crucial traits in this encounter that speak to us today: a willing and obedient spirit, virtue, courage, and selflessness.

We know very little about Mary's upbringing or her family. We do know that Mary had *already* found favor with God (Luke 1:28). We can surmise that she had established a life pattern of obedience—a habit of doing what was right—even when it meant facing certain difficulty.

Consider the significance of Mary's name. It is derived from the Hebrew root word *marah,* meaning "bitter." The book of Exodus tells the story of how Moses and the people of Israel crossed the Red Sea (Exodus 15:22–25). Fleeing from the Egyptians, they spent three days in the wilderness without water. The account reports that they came to *Marah,* but they couldn't drink the water there for it was bitter with harsh minerals. The Lord told Moses to throw a branch of a certain tree into the water, and its chemical action neutralized the minerals, making the water sweet so the people could drink.[4]

In a similar way, Mary's call would be bittersweet. The bitterness of our sins would be taken away as Jesus, the tender young branch springing from the root of Jesse, brought sweet salvation to thirsting mankind (Isaiah 11:10).

Like Moses', Mary's call was altogether focused, singular. She was to be a spiritual pioneer, leading people to the One who gives the water of life. Yet she does not appear to have been waiting around, postponing her chores and daydreaming about a life filled with excitement or far-flung adventure. How often do we despise our everyday tasks, anticipating something more, something better? Even our spiritual lives can be colored by desires for more intense religious experiences, a higher position, or more honor.

We know, too, that in Mary's day, parents cultivated in their children the habits of godly obedience. There were annual feasts, the pilgrimages to Jerusalem to witness the temple sacrifice. And every Friday, before sundown, Mary would have joined in the Sabbath with the women and other girls—sweeping the houses free of leaven, preparing food for the coming day of rest when no work could be done, hauling extra pots of water, cleaning out mildew, filling oil lamps, trimming wicks—habitually at work keeping the light of God's Word alive in every fiber of their lives.

Does this "spiritual patterning" have anything to say to us today? I believe that in our roles as godly parents, nothing matters more than making faith a part of our everyday lives. Not just in outward habits—important as they are—but as we cooperate with God, so that our personal lives become examples to our children, displaying from within the fruit of the Spirit: love, joy, peace, patience, kindness, goodness, faithfulness, gentleness, and self-control (Galatians 5:22).

I do not think it is farfetched to say that the "light" Mary bore within her—which brought her favor with God—was cultivated by a whole culture that was aimed toward godliness. Sexually, Mary had been kept in a state of purity—a state that has fallen out of fashion in this age of the sexual revolution. How sad that virginity is viewed as old-fashioned, when its value is becoming increasingly apparent with the spread of AIDS and other sexually transmitted diseases. Virginity needs to be seen for its positive value: It is an acknowledgment of self-worth, not a sacrifice.

Too often, though, we idealize New Testament times—and for that matter any bygone generation—believing that lax moral standards are unique to our day. But if chastity was the norm in those days, then the Bible would not deal so frequently, and so sternly, with adultery and prostitution.

Mary's virginity mattered, and it was not a cultural given. An article from _Moody Monthly_ points out, "Mary demonstrated a purity that grows out of a modest and godly life. The village of Nazareth, where she grew up, lay in the path of the caravans that traveled from Capernaum to the seaports. As in every generation, there were women in that town who involved themselves with the traveling men. But not Mary—Mary was pure."[5]

Reflecting on Mary's moral excellence, it is important to note that in the Old Testament, "virtue" and "valor" are translated from the same Hebrew word, _chayil_.[6] Apparently, it was translated "valor" when describing men, and "virtue" when referring to women. It is derived from the root word _chiyl,_ which pertains to "bearing and bringing forth," perhaps requiring time and indicating pain and effort in the process—a moral travail. Mary's life exemplifies this trait consistently throughout all the New Testament references to her.

Mary's courage in saying yes to God is an example beyond rival. She knew her life could be in danger. The marriage arranged by her family and Joseph's family would be jeopardized. Her family most likely would not understand. Her reputation would be compromised. Her circumstances would become peculiar, to say the least.

Mary appears to have possessed a quiet, gentle spirit, yet a tremendous strength. Her submission arose from a humble heart. She combined meekness and might. Content to walk in paths God chose for her, she was also courageous in accepting the worldly shame her choice promised to bring her.

Mary's willingness before God reflects her character. Many modern psychologists and sociologists theorize the impact of heredity and circumstances on our development as individuals. Yet these factors do not ultimately determine character. Our personal choices establish character. Judging by her attitude, it is easy to imagine that Mary had habitually chosen to live in a manner that pleased God. Likewise, we must make right decisions about our direction *before* temptation lures us to choose evil.

For any woman who struggles against low self-esteem, or feels left out of things the world considers important, remember this: God chose to share the greatest secret of all creation with a woman. The Father chose one of "our kind" for this honor and trusted her with great responsibility. This speaks clearly of the value and worth of women in His sight and in His plans.

So many Christian women long for female role models. They are looking for heroines. Why not look at the purity of Mary? The Father chose her, and we can choose her, too, as we seek biblical models of women who lived in ways that pleased God. We need the same willing heart as Mary—a heart that says to the Lord, "May it be to me as you have said!"

Questions to Ponder

1. If God spoke to me today, would I be ready to hear Him? Would I listen with ears of faith? How would I respond?

2. How can I best prepare my children to have a willing, God-centered spirit?

3. Is there anything in my life today that would prevent me from receiving a specific call from God and saying yes to it?

4. In what ways does Mary's example speak to my circumstances?

*A*t that time Mary got ready and hurried to a town in the hill country of Judah, where she entered Zechariah's home and greeted Elizabeth. When Elizabeth heard Mary's greeting, the baby leaped in her womb, and Elizabeth was filled with the Holy Spirit.

In a loud voice she exclaimed: "Blessed are you among women, and blessed is the child you will bear! But why am I so favored, that the mother of my Lord should come to me? As soon as the sound of your greeting reached my ears, the baby in my womb leaped for joy. Blessed is she who has believed that what the Lord has said to her will be accomplished!"

And Mary said: "My soul praises the Lord and my spirit rejoices in God my Savior, for he has been mindful of the humble state of his servant. From now on all generations will call me blessed, for the Mighty One has done great things for me—holy is his name.

"His mercy extends to those who fear him, from generation to generation. He has performed mighty deeds with his arm; he has scattered those who are proud in their inmost thoughts.

"He has brought down rulers from their thrones but has lifted up the humble. He has filled the hungry with good things but has sent the rich away empty. He has helped his servant Israel, remembering to be merciful to Abraham and his descendants forever, even as he said to our fathers."

Mary stayed with Elizabeth for about three months and then returned home.

LUKE 1:39–56

3

Celebrating Truth: Woman to Woman

EIN KEREM IS THE SITE in Israel where Mary and Elizabeth are believed to have greeted each other, both in wonder at the news of their pregnancies and filled with praise for God. It lies just west of Jerusalem in an area green with vegetation and terraced hillsides. Noticeably less barren and harsh than the Israeli desert, Ein Kerem means "vineyard spring," its very name hinting of new life.

When my daughter and I arrived at Ein Kerem, we stopped at a church that is said to mark the home of the priest Zechariah and his wife, Elizabeth. From there we drove up a twisting, steeply graded road on the outskirts of town. Confused by guidebooks, I asked our guide why Zechariah and Elizabeth appeared to have two homes. She explained that according to tradition, priests such as Zechariah were well paid. He and his wife could afford to have a residence in town as well as a more secluded home high in the nearby hills. Since Scripture records that Elizabeth secluded herself for five months, perhaps she had gone up to the second site, not receiving anyone until she entered her last trimester.

We drove as far up the steep hill as we could go, left the car behind, and continued up the incline on foot. We finally arrived, puffing and perspiring, at the Shrine of the Visitation. Layers of small hills stretched before us like irregular ridges on an old-fashioned scrubboard. Tinted green with new growth, the ridges were a mid-summer oddity. Most of Israel was dry and brown.

The Shrine of the Visitation, originally built in 1674, houses ancient ruins. Enclosed in the church is a crypt purported to be from the original home of Zechariah and Elizabeth.

As I stood in the quiet courtyard, a soft wind rustled the leaves of the trees. What an ideal spot for that mystical meeting Luke recorded. Two holy and privileged women—one seemingly too old to be pregnant, one seemingly too young—each carried a baby who would change humankind's future. One would announce the coming of the world's Savior; the other *was* that Savior.

Mary had learned about Elizabeth's miraculous pregnancy from Gabriel. I imagine that Mary, like any woman pregnant for the first time, yearned for a friend with whom she could share all the emotional and physical changes to come. And she undoubtedly wanted to see for herself what God had done. Had He really brought new life to Elizabeth's barren womb, as the angel had said? Clearly, it was true. God provided a faith-builder for young Mary, and the companionship of someone who uniquely understood Mary's own circumstance.

We can only guess what Mary told her family and how she arranged the trip. Surely she didn't travel alone. Possibly some relatives who also knew Elizabeth traveled along by donkey or on foot. No matter who accompanied her, the journey was arduous, taking up to ten days along the routes of that day. The group may have crossed the Jordan River to the east, then crossed back to the west, perhaps near Jericho. Although it lengthened the trip, Jewish people often followed this route to avoid traveling south through Samaria, for Samaria was held in contempt. It was not an easy trip.

That afternoon in Ein Kerem, I stood in the serenity of that special church courtyard, contemplating Mary's response to Elizabeth's greeting. Her divinely inspired song of praise is recorded in forty-one languages on the yard's mosaic walls. Catholics call her beautiful canticle the Magnificat, using the first word in its Latin translation. Magnificat means "magnify," and Mary begins her song by saying, as it is sometimes translated, "My soul magnifies the Lord." Once again, she did not focus on herself, but enlarged upon the wonderful ways God had demonstrated His faithfulness through the ages. It is assumed that Mary sang the Magnificat, for it echoes the spontaneous songs of the Hebrew people in Old Testament tradition.

Her triumphant song speaks of God's mercy, His might, and fidelity. Above all, the Magnificat reveals that Mary was a devout Jewish girl who loved Israel's God, revered His Covenant, and believed in His faithful love. Mary quotes the barren Hannah's prayer recorded in First Samuel. She quotes the Psalms four times, and refers to two promises from Exodus and Genesis—apparently because she had pondered God's Word, hiding it in her heart.

How did Mary learn the Word of God? This was not an obvious question to me, until I learned that education was not common among women then. Rabbis did not approve of girls being instructed as boys were. Their usual work consisted of household chores and child rearing. "Women are of little mind" was an often-repeated phrase then—a widely accepted tenet of the common wisdom.[1]

Some have suggested that lowly Nazareth just might have afforded unusual learning opportunities for girls like Mary. It was a center where priests were stationed and would gather before going together to the Temple in Jerusalem. Some stayed behind, spending time fasting and praying for the others.[2] It is possible that the priests' presence in a place such as Nazareth would have a profound impact on people who took their faith seriously. Perhaps Mary and her family were influenced by the priests' study of the Scriptures. Whether or not Mary learned them in a formal setting, the Holy Spirit quickened words of Scripture in this young mind. And now the Word was alive in her very flesh!

Do we women fully consider the preciousness of life— of each individual life we house within our bodies for nine months? Mary probably did not realize the full significance of her call to "house" the Son of God in her womb, to give Him a dwelling place of muscle, blood, and bone. The Catholic church refers to Mary as the "Second Ark of the Covenant." In the Old Testament, the Ark of the Covenant was a chest containing, among other things, the two tablets of the Law given by God to the Israelites. The Ark was carried about by the ancient Hebrews, and it was considered to contain the very presence of God. Scholars differ over whether or not Luke's account of Mary specifically reflects the symbolism of the Ark of the Covenant. Yet they agree that there are some striking parallels between two key scriptural accounts:

> Mary is told, "The power of the Most High will

overshadow you." The same verb is used when the cloud of God's glory overshadows the Tabernacle in the desert . . . and when the winged cherubim overshadow the Ark of the Covenant. . . . In Luke 1:43, as Elizabeth greets Mary, she says, "But why am I so favored, that the mother of my Lord should come to me?" In 2 Samuel 6:9 David says, "How can the Ark of the Lord come to me?" At the visitation Mary remains with Elizabeth about three months (Luke 1:56); the Ark of the Covenant remained three months in the house of Obededom (2 Samuel 6:11).[3]

I first encountered this comparison at the site of Abinadab's house on a hill in the old city of Kiriath-jearim, near Jerusalem. The house no longer exists, but it is mentioned in 1 and 2 Samuel. It harbored the Ark of the Covenant for twenty years after the Philistines returned it to Israel.

A very old, sleepy church now marks the traditional site. The interior was empty and appeared desolate, its walls, floors, and exterior walkways were cracked and flaking away. The sense of biblical history stirred me, though, since the activity and commercialism of so many other tourist sites were absent here. I stood for some time outside the rear of the church and gazed at a unique replacement for the traditional church steeple. It was a large statue of a quite pregnant Mary standing atop the Ark of the Covenant.

The church is called the Church of the Second Ark.

Consider the symbolism. The Ark held God's presence. And now Mary carried God incarnate in her womb. The Ark contained the tablets of the Law. Mary held the Lawgiver. The Ark held Aaron's rod of authority. Mary carried the One who held authority over all things in heaven and on earth. The Ark held the jar of manna—the bread of God's provision to sustain the Hebrew people in the wilderness. Mary bore Jesus, the "Bread of Life."

In a sense, Christians are all "arks" of His presence, temples of God's Holy Spirit. He chooses us, guides us, provides for us, and gives us authority in Him. In Mary, we find a unique and startling example of the *first* believer to "carry" Jesus, who is the very presence of God among us. As believers, we grow in awe and in praise of God as the reality of His presence in our lives takes hold. Think how it must have been for Mary!

Sharing the news of her miraculous pregnancy with another woman similarly blessed must have helped Mary grasp and appreciate the magnificence of God. Imagine what it must have been like when she and Elizabeth first encountered each other.

Heart to Heart

"Mary, slow down!" a traveling companion shouted. The young girl's face was flushing from the difficult climb, not to mention the preceding tedious days spent on the back of a donkey. Mary practically bounded up the final few stone steps to the doorway of her cousin's retreat at Ein Kerem.

"Elizabeth—are you here?" Mary called out as she knocked. She had to see the miracle for herself. And there was Elizabeth, old enough to be Mary's mother, if not her grandmother, visibly pregnant and due to deliver in another few months. For years, she and Zechariah had longed for a baby. And now, in God's amazing timing, one was on the way.

Mary saw how Elizabeth's face had begun to line with

age—*But she glows!* Mary mused. *She looks much younger than I remember.* The two women embraced.

"As soon as the sound of your greeting reached my ears," Elizabeth whispered, "the baby in my womb leaped for joy."

Elizabeth confirmed to Mary that God's call on her life was indeed real. Being the wife of a priest, seasoned in years, Elizabeth offered reassurance. She too was knowledgeable about prophecies concerning the coming Messiah, and she marveled at God's faithfulness after so many years of silence. Here! Now! God was preparing a path of salvation. And this diminutive woman before her—her little cousin Mary—was selected to bear the coming Savior!

"Blessed is she who has believed that what the Lord has said to her will be accomplished!" Elizabeth told her. Mary felt all the tensions of her hard journey melt away. Relaxed and comforted by her cousin, she began a spontaneous song of praise, putting new words to a timeless Hebrew melody:

"My soul praises the Lord and my spirit rejoices in God my Savior, for he has been mindful of the humble state of his servant. From now on all generations will call me blessed, for the Mighty One has done great things for me—holy is his name."

Later they shared a meal of bread and fish. Mary was full of questions. She'd told as few people as possible about her pregnancy. Now, with Elizabeth, her pent-up concerns spilled out. She wondered aloud about midwives and labor, about caring for a newborn and, eventually, a young boy—keeping him safe from disease and injuries. Together they marveled at God's power and might—at the ways in which His hand had silently, powerfully redirected the course of their lives.

She and Elizabeth talked in hushed voices about the angel's message. Gabriel had appeared to Zechariah, not to Elizabeth, and he had imparted a message about God's plan for the child Elizabeth carried. "The angel said my son will bring many of the people of Israel back to the Lord," Elizabeth told Mary. "He said this child will 'make ready a people prepared for the Lord.' "

Mary contemplated this, thinking of the new life within her own flesh. "He said my child will 'ascend the throne of David and reign forever,' He will be called 'the Son of the Most High.' " For a long while they talked, recalling the Scriptures' teachings about a coming King who would restore the throne of Israel. The sun sank behind the hills and oil lamps were lit. This Messiah was thought by many to be a future political leader, one who might wrest control of Israel back from Herod and the grip of Rome.

"Somehow," Elizabeth concluded, "the purposes of God are going to be fulfilled by these two boys. We cannot know how this will happen. We must only trust God. But we must raise these children in keeping with what God has revealed. They must be trained in the Scriptures, obedient to their fathers, and treated normally—not overprotected or overly indulged."

Mary was tiring now, yet was spiritually recharged. It was late when she settled herself on the sleeping mat Elizabeth laid out for her. She gazed into the pale moonlight, faintly illuminating the fresh air coming in through the open window. Sleep came only with great difficulty since this beautiful yet frightening adventure had begun. Pulling her cloak over her shoulders, she whispered, half to herself, half in prayer, "I am so grateful to be with a woman who understands. Thank you for that kindness." And tears came. "My spirit soared when Elizabeth greeted me—my heart overflows with love for you! How I love you, my God. . . ."

There were difficulties, serious concerns about the future, and uncertainties back in Nazareth, including Joseph, her family, and all the details of raising a child born out of wedlock. Surely a God who could perform the wonders she had already seen would take care of those things, too. It was as if, in trusting all her difficulties to Him, she was able to fall asleep in His arms.

Walking a Difficult Way

The brief New Testament account of Mary's meeting with Elizabeth is rich with messages for women facing difficulties today. Mary sought the companionship of an older, wiser woman who would understand her circumstances. She kept her focus on God and His purposes, and did not get sidetracked by dwelling on herself and the uncertainties of the future. Grounded in the Word of God, Mary knew the value of praise and worship.

Perhaps the most compelling lesson of this passage concerns the relationship between these two women. It would have been perfectly understandable for Mary to remain in the comfort of her home in Nazareth, yet she undertook a strenuous journey to be with Elizabeth.

Isn't it true that when we find ourselves facing unusual or difficult circumstances, we're tempted to withdraw into ourselves, to lapse into self-pity? It is not easy for most of us to reach out and risk rejection or misunderstanding. Yet the Bible exhorts us to do exactly what Mary and Elizabeth did. In Titus 2:4, older women are instructed to "train the younger women to love their husbands and children, to be self-controlled and pure, to be busy at home, to be kind, and to be subject to their husbands. . . ."

What happens when one woman with experience, understanding, and a godly perspective gets to know a younger woman dealing with life's dilemmas? It appears that Elizabeth related to Mary as an equal and not from a position of superiority. In fact, she commented, "Why am I so favored, that the mother of my Lord should come to me?" How uplifting and encouraging!

Elizabeth also offered concrete observations to confirm God's call to Mary, and she acknowledged Mary's strong faith. Can you imagine how good you would feel if a woman you greatly respected treated you the way Elizabeth treated Mary? Today, it is essential to look for ways to build one another up, to encourage one another in our faith walk. This is the kind of spiritual interdependence we all need to fulfill God's purposes for our lives.

There was a time, a number of years ago, when I felt overwhelmed by the many demands on me and the different directions my future could take. Trying to sort things out was a real challenge, and I knew I needed both spiritual and practical guidance. At the same time, a woman of great spiritual maturity, whom I knew casually, found herself moved to pray for me. She expressed concern for me. We prayed together, and more importantly, she prayed for me. I was amazed to find that she had the objectivity about my life that I was losing hold of, and she encouraged me in certain sensible directions. She was a great help to me, and we have remained good friends.

Are you trying to go it alone, when wise help is what you need? Mary's song, which "magnifies" the Lord, demonstrates that true praise for God wells up from within. The importance of praise is reflected in the meaning of the names in this story. Elizabeth lived in the province of Judah, which means "praise." Mary "came into praise" when she "came into Judah" to visit Elizabeth.

Mary said, "My soul has rejoiced in God my Savior." The soul is the realm of our intellect, will, and emotions. At the same time, the soul is also the spiritual battleground, and when we choose to go against God's Word, it is the seat of rebellion. As Christians, we have the privilege of modeling our lives after Mary, by submitting our logic, self-will, and feelings to God and to His Word.

A. Moody Stuart, a Scottish preacher and author of the nineteenth century, wrote eloquently of Mary's words to Elizabeth. Her mention of Abraham and his descendants, Stuart notes, points out her strong allegiance and commitment to her Jewish heritage as well as her familiarity with the Word of God:

> These are not thoughts of the moment in Mary's soul, but must have been the long-cherished aspirations of her heart. Her hopes, like all Israelites, had been concentrated on the great promise, the promised Seed. . . .[4]

Stuart reminds us that Mary was prepared when God called her into service. She knew God's Word and its power, and she hungered after Him and His will. We, too, can pattern our own daily devotion to God after Mary's, as we prepare for whatever He has for us. The importance of this kind of preparation is indeed timeless.

Mary's words reflect her love and devotion to God. They also illustrate her view of herself, and this perspective is particularly significant today when society bombards women with slogans glorifying worldly success, achievement, and self-promotion. In the Magnificat Mary takes exactly the opposite view: She acknowledges herself as one of "humble state," a lowly one. Theologians believe she represents the *anawim*, Israel's "poor ones":

> The term may have originally designated the ec-
> onomically poor (and frequently still included them),
> but it came to refer more widely to those who could
> not trust in their own strength: the downtrodden, the
> poor, the lowly, the afflicted, the widows, and or-
> phans. The opposite of the *anawim* were not simply
> the rich, but the proud and self-sufficient who trusted
> in their own strength and showed no need for God.[5]

Mary certainly represented Israel's faithful and humble,
all those who seemed insignificant. In the world's eyes she
was powerless and ordinary—yet in the eyes of eternity
there was nothing insignificant about her. She was the
human vessel that would robe humankind's Savior in flesh!

God's will for Mary and for Elizabeth involved something many of us take for granted: entering into the world
of motherhood. Not every woman is so blessed. In this
biblical vignette, God shows himself to be the God of the
womb. Elizabeth and Zechariah, according to the passage
in Luke, "were upright in the sight of God, observing all
the Lord's commandments and regulations blamelessly"
(Luke 1:6). Even though barrenness was viewed as a
curse—as evidence of something wrong in an individual's
life—Scripture is clear: Inability to bear children is no reflection of a person's worth in God's sight.

Unfortunately, misunderstandings about infertility
persist even among Christians today. There are some who
question a woman's faithfulness in prayer or obedience if
she has difficulty conceiving a child. Friends who have
experienced infertility tell me it is common for others to
blame the condition on emotional problems rather than
physical limitations. Surely the biblical account of God

moving in Elizabeth's life offers a more compassionate view of barrenness.

Mary's experience also speaks to those who *do* become pregnant, in the way she cherished the life developing within her. As we will see in the chapters that follow, she was diligent in her role as a mother. That was her primary calling in life, and she remained devoted to it. She models for us a refreshing contrast to current views that devalue child rearing, that see it as a burden, not a blessing.

To me, this passage about Mary and Elizabeth also speaks to one of the central moral issues of our day: abortion. These days, a woman in Mary's circumstances might be considered to have a "crisis pregnancy." Tragically, in our present-day controversy concerning unborn children, the womb has become a battleground. Some people support legalized abortion, defending what many of them sincerely believe are women's rights. They don't believe that abortion takes the life of a baby, because they believe that before birth it's only a lump of tissue. Some insist that no one knows when life really begins. They call the developing baby an embryo, and then, as it develops, a fetus. Not until it exits the womb does it deserve to be called a baby. The Scriptures disagree. Psalm 139 tells us that life begins at conception. The ultimate example is the story of Mary and Elizabeth.

When Mary visited Elizabeth, the embryo in her womb was no more than a few weeks into development. Yet Elizabeth's six-month-old fetus recognized Mary's barely developed embryo. God ordained that a six-month-old fetus would bear witness to the coming of the world's Savior! This account vividly illustrates that Jesus was alive in His mother's womb from the moment of conception.

In all these areas, our commitment as Christians can

be strengthened as we let our hearts dwell on the encounter between Mary and Elizabeth.

Because the life that is centered in spiritual commitment can be lonely, we need to seek companionship. We need one another. We need the same kind of fellowship Mary and Elizabeth shared—time together that uplifts, encourages, and empowers us to go on. Together, we can celebrate the Lord's goodness and encourage one another in faith. When we do, our souls leap with joy and find new strength.

Questions to Ponder

1. Who are the women in my life who can encourage me and strengthen my faith? To whom could I offer the same sort of blessing?
2. Do I believe, as Mary did, that what the Lord has promised will be accomplished?
3. In my times of worship to the Lord, how may I better reflect the attitude of humility, devotion, and praise seen in the Magnificat?
4. How does the meeting between Mary and Elizabeth inform my thinking about abortion?

*I*n those days Caesar Augustus issued a decree that a census should be taken of the entire Roman world. . . . And everyone went to his own town to register. So Joseph also went up from the town of Nazareth in Galilee of Judea, to Bethlehem, the town of David, because he belonged to the house and line of David. He went there to register with Mary, who was pledged to be married to him and was expecting a child.

While they were there, the time came for the baby to be born, and she gave birth to her firstborn, a son. She wrapped him in cloths and placed him in a manger, because there was no room for them in the inn.

And there were shepherds living out in the fields nearby, keeping watch over their flocks at night. An angel of the Lord appeared to them, and the glory of the Lord shone around them, and they were terrified.

But the angel said to them, "Do not be afraid. I bring you good news of great joy that will be for all the people. Today in the town of David a Savior has been born to you; he is Christ the Lord. This will be a sign to you: You will find a baby wrapped in cloths and lying in a manger."

Suddenly a great company of the heavenly host appeared with the angel, praising God and saying, "Glory to God in the highest, and on earth peace to men on whom his favor rests."

When the angels had left them and gone into heaven, the shepherds said to one another, "Let's go to Bethlehem and see this thing that has happened, which the Lord has told us about."

LUKE 2:1–15

4

A Son Is Given

ONCE A YEAR, CHRISTIANS all around the world turn their eyes to Bethlehem. It is one of the world's most unlikely places to attract worldwide attention: a small, dusty Arab town situated in the hills of Judea, six miles south of Jerusalem. Its streets are a scramble of steep grades and sharp curves. It is home to many Arab Christians, and their churches dot the town along with schools, houses, and workshops. Carved olive-wood figurines depicting the Nativity are sold all over town. From Bethlehem, a visitor can gaze out over fields where shepherds still watch their flocks by night. Once a year, when we are singing about Bethlehem, thousands of believers gather there to celebrate the birth of Jesus, and millions more watch television images beamed around the globe by satellite, recalling the events of the first Christmas.

On a cool, clear night, I stood in Bethlehem's Manger Square. It was Christmas Eve, and I was packed in among the throngs who had come to celebrate the birth of Jesus. How very different Bethlehem must have appeared to Mary on the evening when she arrived, her stomach taut with child, her body aching with the onset of labor. The village was overcrowded then, too—but completely indifferent to Mary, her pain, and her needs.

Why had God selected such an out-of-the-way location for the birth of His Son? Why had He made it so inconvenient for Mary and Joseph, sending a nine-months-pregnant woman on an arduous trip by donkey? I wonder if Mary and Joseph felt they had already experienced enough personal turmoil to last a lifetime.

Bethlehem was the market town for the tribe of Judah, the home of Ruth and Boaz, and the birthplace of King David. Bethlehem was called Ephrath, or Ephrathah, until after Joshua's conquest of Canaan. Its new name, Bethlehem, means "House of Bread." It is the place chosen by God and foretold by prophets to be the birthplace of Jesus, humankind's "Bread of Life."

Little Bethlehem appeared insignificant. Yet more than seven hundred years before Jesus' birth, the prophet Micah wrote: "But you, Bethlehem Ephrathah, though you are small among the clans of Judah, out of you will come for me one who will be ruler over Israel, whose origins are from of old from ancient times. Therefore, Israel will be abandoned until the time when she who is in labor gives birth" (Micah 5:2–3).

Israel had two Bethlehems in ancient days—one in Judah and the other in Galilee (see 1 Samuel 16:4; Joshua 19:15). Micah's precise prophecy identified the very one accorded the honor of being the birthplace of God's Son.

Someone had warned me about the circus-like atmosphere that takes over the normally quiet square next to the Church of the Nativity on contemporary Christmas Eves. The laughter and jostling that chilly evening seemed at odds with the event we had come to celebrate.

As the crowd poured into the church for evening services, Roger and I stood elbow-to-elbow with tourists and pilgrims in the Roman Catholic section of the large church complex. I recalled watching that unique Mass on other Christmas Eves in the United States, as it was broadcast by television to millions around the world. On the night we were there, the stuffy air inside the church and the insulation of my warm coat made me light-headed. I decided to leave the sanctuary before the service ended, and Roger came with me.

The Basilica of the Nativity is divided into several sections, and stooping to step through a small door, Roger and I found ourselves in the cavernous sanctuary of the church's Orthodox section. A handful of people, mostly Greek priests in their black vestments and long gray beards, gravitated toward a stairway beside the central altar area. Light rose from the base of the stone steps and we made our way down on tiptoe, so as not to disturb those in meditative silence.

At the bottom of the steps, we entered the very place I would have chosen to be that Christmas Eve—a small, ornately decorated grotto. Here a single golden star is set in the marble floor to mark the spot where tradition says Mary bore her infant son. We joined with several others from a variety of different countries, breathing a holy ambiance enhanced by incense and candles. As we stood there worshiping, several Armenian nuns knelt and quietly sang before the manger area.

I have never forgotten that special Christmas Eve.

When Roger and I left the grotto, we wandered out into a small courtyard. Church bells rang the midnight call. The night winds rustled the leaves of the trees.

Is this what Mary heard the night Jesus was born? Did the wind blow softly then, too? I wondered. That momentous event seemed far removed from today's world—removed as well from the revelry of the modern-day crowd marking the holiday in Bethlehem. Yet it happened to real flesh-and-blood people—Mary and Joseph. . . .

Because they were betrothed, Mary was legally considered Joseph's wife, and so she was compelled by law to go to Bethlehem with him. At the time, Israel had suffered Roman domination for some sixty years. The authorities demanded a census for Rome's methodical tax system, and every family had to travel to the town of its ancestors: The system accepted no excuses.

Up to this point in the Gospel narratives, little has been said about Joseph. What about this man Mary was engaged to marry? A carpenter, Joseph probably learned his trade from his father and planned to carry on the family business after he had a wife and family of his own. Everything in his life seemed to be going along successfully and uneventfully. And now this!

When Joseph had discovered Mary's pregnancy, he initially reacted as any man would: He assumed his bride-to-be had been unfaithful. Yet he did not lash out in anger. Matthew notes that he was "a righteous man" who did not want to disgrace Mary, so he intended to divorce her quietly. John MacArthur makes these observations about Joseph:

> For the very reason that he was a righteous man, Joseph had a double problem, at least in his own mind. First, because of his righteous moral standards,

he knew that he should not go through with the marriage because of Mary's pregnancy. He knew that he was not the father, and assumed, quite naturally, that Mary had had relations with another man. But second, because of his righteous love and kindness, he could not bear the thought of shaming her publicly (a common practice of his day in regard to such an offense), much less demand her death, as provided by the law (Deuteronomy 22:23–24). There is no evidence that Joseph felt anger, resentment, or bitterness. He had been shamed (if what he assumed was true), but his concern was not for his own shame but for Mary's.[1]

But after he had considered this, an angel of the Lord appeared to him in a dream and said, "Joseph son of David, do not be afraid to take Mary home as your wife, because what is conceived in her is from the Holy Spirit. She will give birth to a son, and you are to give him the name Jesus, because he will save his people from their sins." (Matthew 1:20–21).

Matthew makes a point to tell us that Joseph awoke and obeyed the angel's command at once. It is important to note that an engagement, or betrothal, was in some respects even more significant than the actual marriage ceremony in those times. The betrothal signaled the successful closure of negotiations between the fathers of the bride and groom. It was legally binding; the husband-to-be took legal possession of the wife. She then belonged to him, not to her father. Yet physical consummation of the relationship was strictly prohibited until after a second ceremony that celebrated the new marriage.

There is no indication of when Joseph and Mary had a marriage ceremony, or if they had one. Perhaps they chose to be married in a quiet, private manner because of the circumstances. In any event, Joseph was faithful to the regulations of Israel and to the instructions God gave him in the dream. Matthew notes that Joseph "kept her a virgin until she gave birth to a son" (1:25). Joseph was indeed a righteous man, who knew and honored his high call from the Lord.

The Nazarene couple probably arrived unnoticed in busy Bethlehem that evening. It didn't help that Joseph and Mary were despised Galileans, simple hill-folks who were disdained by most Jews. All those people from various walks of Jewish life who had gathered in Bethlehem— among them religious leaders educated in the Scriptures— missed a fantastic opportunity. The religious crowd, the innkeepers, the merchants and workers—all were unsympathetic on that night we call Christmas Eve. God came to them, and they were so busy that they never even noticed. They never expected this Promised One, the Messiah, to come to them in a humble manner, and so they missed Him!

In _The Hungering Dark_, Frederick Buechner describes the meaning of Christ's unexpected birth:

> The Christ child born in the night among beasts. The sweet breath and steaming dung of beasts. And nothing is ever the same again.
>
> Those who believe in God can never be sure of Him again. Once they have seen God in a stable, they can never be sure where He will appear, to what lengths God will go or to what ludicrous depths of self-humiliation God will descend in the wild pursuit of humankind.
>
> If holiness and the awful power and majesty of God were present in this least auspicious of all events, this birth of a peasant's child, then there is no place or time so lowly and earthbound but that holiness

can be present there too.

And this means that we are never safe, that there is no place where we can hide from God. There is no place where we are safe from His power to break in two and re-create the human heart. It is just where God seems most helpless that God is most strong. It is just where we least expect Him that He comes most fully.[2]

Surely Bethlehem was the last place people expected to encounter God-become-man, God in the form of a helpless baby, 2,000 years ago. What might have happened on the evening Mary and Joseph arrived?

A Miracle Baby

The sky began to grow darker as Joseph and Mary neared Bethlehem. They had been on the road from Nazareth for days, Mary settled somewhat awkwardly on the back of a donkey and Joseph leading, holding the reins. "We're almost there," Joseph said over his shoulder.

From where she sat, Mary could see the box-like houses of Bethlehem clustered on the horizon. "We'll go to the inn first and get a room there," Joseph continued. Masking his own qualms about the night ahead, he tried his best to comfort and reassure Mary.

The crush of people entering Bethlehem was worse than Joseph imagined, and he resigned himself to a stop-and-go plod into town. With an eye to the dwindling sunlight in the west he wondered, *Where will all these people find lodging?* He shook his head in frustration over the oppressive Roman laws to which his people were subject. Not even a full-term pregnancy was enough to exempt Mary from appearing on the day appointed for the census.

As they waited in line outside the inn, the couple shared a meal they'd packed from home—small loaves of bread, dried fish, grapes and figs. At last it was Joseph's turn to request a room. "The inn is full," the innkeeper told him abruptly. "There are no rooms left."

"My wife is expecting a baby," Joseph pressed him.

When it was clear Joseph would not take "no" for an answer, the innkeeper gestured toward the back of the building. "There's a stable out back. It's yours for the night."

Without a word, Joseph led his young wife around back to the stable. Smoothing his cloak over a pad of clean straw, he could tell Mary was in pain. "The baby is coming," she said, wincing as she positioned herself slowly onto the bed of straw.

At last, Mary's baby boy emerged into the world, red-wrinkled and crying. Mary fell back against the straw, exhausted, caressing her little boy for the first time. She could not take her eyes off the delicate nose and mouth, and she whispered a prayer of wonder and thanks: "Lord, my spirit rejoices in you. You have fulfilled your promise! I can touch the One the angel foretold. He lies here beside me—this little son."

Mary leaned on her elbow and pulled her long hair aside, positioning herself so the yellow moonlight flickering in the stable door could touch her infant's face. So tiny—so helpless. *How can I care for your precious Son? What do you have planned for Him? O my God, you must help me!*

Then she caught sight of Joseph, standing at the stable door, staring into the distance. . . .

The sky above the pasturelands outside Bethlehem suddenly glowed as if a million candles had all come alight at the same moment. *A thunderstorm?* Joseph wondered. *No, that wasn't thunder,* he decided. Then what was the sound that rang down from the sky?

It seemed as though Joseph heard voices in the distance—a multitude of harmonies blending beautifully together. Joseph walked to Mary's side now and crouched beside her and the baby, who had begun to nurse at his mother's breast.

"Isn't He perfect?" Mary whispered.

Several of the animals inside the stable began to stir, nudging the door and lowing softly. When Joseph turned his head, he saw a knot of shepherds standing just outside, murmuring among themselves. "What do you want?" Joseph asked, standing.

"The Lord sent us," one shepherd said simply, stepping into the doorway. "The sky lit up like day and an angel appeared! He told us a Savior had been born, and that we would find Him wrapped in cloths and lying in a manger. Then a crowd of angels filled the sky. They were singing: 'Glory to God in highest, and on earth peace to men on whom his favor rests.' "

Joseph allowed the visitors to come in, two at a time, to kneel before the mother and Child. One old man kept shaking his head, as though bewildered by what he was seeing. Mary clasped his hand to assure him. "An angel appeared to me, too," she said. "He told me that this baby will rule as our King one day—in a kingdom that will never end. It must be true."

Quietly the shepherds left the stable, wandering back to their flocks beneath a sky that seemed changed after such a heavenly celebration. And Mary finally slept, lulled by the steady breathing of the infant, comforted by the tight clutch of his grip around her forefinger.

Humanity and Divinity

Today, the Christmas story is so familiar to us that it's easy to overlook all the facets of encouragement and challenge it contains. So often, our Christmases are focused on the events following Jesus' birth. But what was going on just before that pivotal event? What was it like for Mary and Joseph as they sought to walk in obedience through a multitude of hardships?

Back in Nazareth, it must have been obvious by the time of the census that Mary was very pregnant. Because they had to travel to Bethlehem in obedience to the law, Mary could not choose to seclude herself protectively from comments and sidelong glances and all the shame a woman feels when others question her character.

Before embarking on the trip, it is possible that Mary was ostracized in her hometown because of the premature pregnancy. Throughout His life, the terminology some would use to describe her son meant "illegitimate" in contemporary English. Years later, Jesus was driven out of the synagogue in Nazareth. He said to the people, as they chased him out of town, "no prophet is accepted in his home town" (Luke 4:24).

The shame Mary endured in Nazareth may not have been so different from what is experienced today by some women who are in crisis pregnancies. How would we have treated Mary and her family? If we envision her as a young girl in a predicament, it may open new space in our heart and a new desire to show compassion to women in need. Without approving of wrong choices they may have made, we nonetheless can reach out with the truth of God's love and care for every individual. It is so easy today for women to choose abortion. Those who do not, and who may opt to raise their children without the support and help of a husband, are greatly in need of our compassion.

Mary's situation was, of course, very different. She was not pregnant because of a transgression, but by God's sovereign action in her life. And she was blessed with a caring husband who consistently placed her needs ahead of his own reputation and ego. Together, Joseph and Mary present a portrait of mutual respect and concern. From the moment Joseph learned of Mary's condition, he apparently considered the consequences she would face depending on what he decided to do. He planned to divorce her quietly, to spare her any public spectacle or punishment. When the angel appeared to him, telling him to remain faithful to Mary as her betrothed husband, he responded with unquestioning obedience.

Beyond the scant New Testament account, the traditions that have accumulated ever since picture Mary as serene and trusting on that tumultuous pathway to Bethlehem. Can you imagine the natural inclination of a tired, pregnant woman whose husband tells her there is no bed for her to sleep in, apart from a pad of straw in a barn? Yet there is no suggestion that she dissolved into tearful frustration or anger. Could it be that, in part, her calm spirit came from knowing God had given her a husband she could rely on no matter what? Marriages work best when these same principles guide our relationships today: Place your spouse's needs first, trust each other, seek God's plan for your lives together, and build each other up by what you say and do.

We women, especially if we are mothers, can identify with the humanity of Mary's motherhood. When Mary held her baby that first night, she must have marveled at the sweet, innocent face. She undoubtedly wondered as He grew in her womb just what He would look like. Now she could see and touch what the angel had promised.

Mary reflected on the nurturing side of God's nature, as all mothers are called to do. All the natural bonding that occurs between a mother and child no doubt took place between Mary and Jesus. They must have shared an enduring bond of human love, in addition to the love between a Savior and the saved.

What Mary experienced with her firstborn son was unique, one-of-a-kind. Yet we have no reason to doubt that Mary was a person with all the feelings, stresses, temptations, joys, and sorrows known to every woman. If we miss her humanity, we miss the marvelous lessons her life affords as we struggle with our own.

Through Mary, God entered the world in the flesh. Because of God's initiative and Mary's willing obedience, she became the bearer of the Incarnate God. None of us will ever experience the same literal, physical presence of God within us, yet Mary's example is one that can still speak to us. Where does God meet our humanity today— in the life of our nation, our communities, our homes? Just as He came to obscure Bethlehem, to a primitive stable, God meets us today in ways that are unexpected and so very ordinary.

Because His Holy Spirit dwells within believers, God enables us to "embody" Christ to those around us—perhaps to kids in the carpool, or our neighbors, or co-workers at the office. We carry Christ into each interaction we have throughout the day. Are we aware of His presence? Do we invite Him to lead us into conversations and relationships where His presence is sorely needed?

As you consider God's reality in your life, think of the stark contrast between what the religious leaders of Jesus' time were expecting and the way in which God chose to reveal himself. All the leaders of the Jews watched and prayed and studied, anticipating the coming of a Messiah in a blaze of glory. Yet Jesus came in swaddling clothes, lying in a manger: sleeping, fussing, nursing, and needing his diaper changed. In our lives, God may come in ways we least expect Him to. And He may make himself known in unusual ways.

When Jesus was born, God did not announce the event to the religious leaders or to the rich and famous. He chose, as He often does, the poor and lowly—the shepherds in the field. Shepherding in the first century was a rough, coarse, nomadic occupation. Yet God sent a birth announcement to common shepherds. And Mary treasured their words, pondering them in her heart.

In the chill of that night, the shepherds watched their flocks in what is now called Shepherd's Field. Light pierced the darkness, and heaven's glory shone around them, interrupting ordinary and mundane duties. They heard angel voices singing in the previously silent night—the first Christmas carolers.

What had those shepherds accomplished to deserve such an honor? Nothing. God simply chose to reveal His great news to them. God shows repeatedly in Scripture that it is not by our merit, but by His choosing that He offers us eternal life.

God honored those men when He called them to see the miracle of the Incarnation. He literally invited them to meet His Son and their Savior. Without hesitation the shepherds accepted. They hurried to the stable to find the baby in a manger. An animal's food bin was transformed into a king's bed. They recognized what God had done, in splendid simplicity, and they worshiped Him.

God offers us that same opportunity to meet His Son and our Savior. The invitation doesn't expire, and it bears an R.S.V.P. How have you responded? Have you personally met Jesus, whom the Father sent because He loves you? Do you need to meet Him afresh?

God arranged for the shepherds to worship the Christ-child that night, to join in heaven's rejoicing. He invites each of us to do the same. As you consider how to respond, keep in mind the Bible's portrayal of Mary—her confidence, courage, and willingness to obey. Temporary pain and inconvenience did not diminish the awe and love and thanks she felt toward God.

Have you accepted the baby Jesus—the sweet child of Bethlehem—and yet neglected to hand over your will to the God who may ask you to follow Him on a difficult path?

God is still speaking today to ordinary women and men, just as He spoke to the common shepherds so long ago. Has He been trying to announce some part of His plan to you? And isn't it worth pondering in your heart?

Questions to Ponder

1. How do I feel toward young women experiencing crisis pregnancies? Is there something I can do to encourage them to honor God by choosing "life"?
2. If I am married, how does Mary teach me to relate to my spouse? What can I do today to cultivate joy, peace, and trust in my marriage?
3. Am I alert for ways God may try to break through into my daily life? When do I sense His presence and how do I respond?
4. Have I taken time to give God my R.S.V.P. to His invitation of eternal life for all who believe in His Son Jesus?

*O*n the eighth day, when it was time to circumcise him, he was named Jesus, the name the angel had given him before he had been conceived.

When the time of their purification according to the Law of Moses had been completed, Joseph and Mary took him to Jerusalem to present him to the Lord (as it is written in the Law of the Lord, "Every firstborn male is to be consecrated to the Lord"), and to offer a sacrifice in keeping with what is said in the Law of the Lord: "a pair of doves or two young pigeons."

Now there was a man in Jerusalem called Simeon, who was righteous and devout. He was waiting for the consolation of Israel, and the Holy Spirit was upon him. It had been revealed to him by the Holy Spirit that he would not die before he had seen the Lord's Christ.

Moved by the Spirit, he went into the temple courts. When the parents brought in the child Jesus to do for him what the custom of the Law required, Simeon took him in his arms and praised God, saying:

"Sovereign Lord, as you have promised, you now dismiss your servant in peace. For my eyes have seen your salvation, which you have prepared in the sight of all people, a light for revelation to the Gentiles and for glory to your people Israel."

The child's father and mother marveled at what was said about him. Then Simeon blessed them and said to Mary, his mother: "This child is destined to cause the falling and rising of many in Israel, and to be a sign that will be spoken against, so that the thoughts of many hearts will be revealed. And a sword will pierce your own soul, too."

LUKE 2:21–35

5

Counting the Cost

MODERN-DAY ISRAEL thrives on its tourist trade, attracting visitors of all sorts from around the world. During my visits there, I have reflected on the different reasons why people might seek out the ancient sites preserved throughout the Holy Land. Some are genuine pilgrims, retracing the steps of Jesus, and perhaps walking the Stations of the Cross in the section of Jerusalem called the Old City. Others seek historic and archeological knowledge, visiting museums and digs. Certainly there are curiosity-seekers with scant interest in spiritual things, and there are those who long for a deeper personal experience of God's presence in their lives.

I came to Israel looking for Mary, wanting to see and touch the places she walked, in search of a multi-faceted sense of who she was and how she lived. I did this in response to an insistent impulse within me concerning Mary—which I recognized as coming from God—not knowing exactly where it would lead.

Immediately, I found myself wondering about the high price Mary was asked to pay, and Joseph too, for the honor of giving flesh and nourishment and a home to God's Son. And I wondered how the cost they paid in following God could instruct me. These questions made me search the Scriptures for further evidence about Jesus' earthly mother and father.

Mary and Joseph were sensitive to God's leading in their lives. Moreover, I found, they were faithful as well to the requirements of the Jewish Law. As they went about fulfilling the laws pertaining to a new child, God had in store certain encounters that both encouraged Mary and Joseph, and prepared them for the challenges of the days ahead. What forms did their simple obedience take?

To begin with, they named their son Jesus and had Him circumcised, in accordance with God's law and the customs of their people. These two ceremonies occurred at the same time according to Luke: eight days after the child's birth. The baby's name had been revealed to Mary, of course, by the angel Gabriel. And to the Israelites, a name carried much deeper significance than it generally does today. A name was thought to reflect an individual's identity; they were an integral part of the person—influencing his character and announcing to others something essential about him. *Jesus* is the Greek form of the Hebrew name, *Joshua*. It means "God is Savior" or "God saves." In Aramaic, the language of everyday conversation in New Testament Palestine, the name was *Yeshua*.

Scripture reveals that God rewarded both Joseph and Mary for their devout prayers, by involving both of them in the naming of Jesus (see Matthew 1:21; Luke 1:31). It says to me that God intends for both parents—mother and father—to take part in the spiritual guidance of their children. And when we commit ourselves to this task, He will come to our aid.

Later in His ministry, Jesus is called *Messiah*, which in Hebrew means "the Anointed." *Christ* is not a surname as some assume, but it is the Greek word for Messiah. During His ministry, He was properly called "Jesus, the Christ." His name holds all the titles that the prophet Isaiah said he would be called—*Emmanuel*: God with us, Prince of Peace, Mighty God, Wonderful Counselor. It is literally, as the old hymn says, a "Name above all names."

Unsettling Words

During her first few weeks as a new mother, Mary found herself thinking ahead to the requirements of the law. Two different rituals must be performed there: a purification rite for Mary and a dedication of the firstborn son. A woman who gave birth was considered ritually unclean by Hebrew law. Approximately forty days after giving birth, the mother was required to bathe herself and offer sacrifices to complete her purification. The rituals of purification and dedication were normally carried out at the local synagogue, and involved paying five shekels of silver to the priest as an acknowledgement that the firstborn belongs to God. But Mary and Joseph went one step further. They took Jesus to Jerusalem. Commentators say their presentation of Jesus was intended to commit Him publicly to the service of the Lord.[1] Apparently the ceremony meant more to them than following a mere custom; it is said to have resembled the overwhelming gratitude of

Hannah presenting Samuel to the Lord (1 Samuel 1:24–28).

As Mary thought about these things, she rejoiced silently over her husband's devotion to her and to Jesus. Throughout the tumultuous months of her pregnancy, Mary had little time to worry about how Joseph would relate to Jesus—how he might feel about raising a child that wasn't his. No matter. Joseph made it clear, in his quiet, steadfast way, that he saw it as an honor to serve as Jesus' earthly father.

Mary wrapped Jesus in a blanket against the evening chill of Bethlehem and settled Him against her shoulder. She walked outside where Joseph was caring for their donkey. When he looked up, a smile spread across his face. "Is the little one still awake?" In the morning, he and Mary would make their way together to the temple at Jerusalem to present Jesus to the Lord, to dedicate Him to God's service. Mary counted herself doubly blessed by this husband, who so patiently put her needs and the needs of their baby ahead of his own.

Their trip to Jerusalem was uneventful—until, at the temple, they encountered an elderly man named Simeon. It was as if he recognized the child, and a light came into the eyes set in that wizened face—along with tears. It was the same joy and wonder Mary had seen in the eyes of the shepherds, except that this old man seemed to know a lot more about Jesus than the shepherds, or even Mary herself. A cloud passed over his face.

Simeon could not take his eyes off the infant. Almost shaking, he lapsed into an enigmatic prayer: "My eyes have seen your salvation, which you have prepared in the sight of all people, a light for revelation to the Gentiles and for glory to your people Israel." Then Simeon turned to face

Mary. "This child is destined to cause the falling and rising of many in Israel, and to be a sign that will be spoken against, so that the thoughts of many hearts will be revealed," he told her. "And a sword will pierce your own soul, too. . . ."

With the hindsight of history, it's easy to forget: Mary knew who Jesus was, but she didn't know what was going to happen to Him—or to herself.

On their way out of Jerusalem, Mary and Joseph traveled in silence. Each felt alone with their private reflections about the marvelous and troubling events that had caught up their once-simple lives. Mary sank into a meditative frame of mind, needing to sort out all she had seen and heard. The baby in her protective arms had fallen asleep from the rocking motion of the donkey. Joseph strode a little ahead and to the animal's side, and Mary could tell by his far-off look that he too was trying to fathom impenetrable questions.

This little boy is meant to do great things, Joseph mused. He returned to the words of Simeon and measured them against the ancient prophecies about the Messiah. *Will Jesus grow up to be a powerful king, to drive out Rome's puppet-kings? Will He be the instigator of a revolution?* Joseph stole a sidelong glance at Jesus, serenely sleeping in Mary's lap. Mary's face gave away her thoughts. *She has many questions, too.*

Mary was turning over the fearful comment Simeon had added. *What does it mean, Lord—a sword will pierce my soul?* Mary blinked away tears of momentary dread. She had gained maturity far beyond that of most girls in their mid-teens, facing so many challenges condensed into these last several months. Gabriel's prophecy seemed so long ago. Yet a whole lifetime of untold events lay ahead. *Holy*

One, her heart cried, *where are you leading us?*

Lord, she continued, *I know who Jesus is because of the way He came to me by your Holy Spirit. Even when it seems impossible, I know this is true. And when the old man held my baby, he knew exactly who Jesus was. I thought I was ready for whatever you have for us, but when that godly man turned to me, with tears in his eyes, and said what would happen, it felt as if his words plunged into my heart. What does it mean?*

Mary looked down at the innocent face, and the tiny fingers that clasped one edge of the blanket. *No matter what happens, help me to be your faithful servant. I will do whatever you ask.*

Had Joseph looked over his shoulder again, he would have seen the tender face of his young wife set itself in a look of firm resolve—a resolve she would need to summon many times in the years ahead.

Persevering Parents

Mary and Joseph were models of faithfulness in their devotion to God and their observance of religious rites. Making the extra effort to take Jesus to the temple at Jerusalem brought the direct confirmation of God's specific call on their lives and on the life of Jesus. What a marvelous example of being in the right place at the right time, by God's grace!

Today, we are called as well to be faithful and consistent in the practice of our Christianity. Our presence at worship services and the Bible classes in our churches turns our attention toward God and affords the opportunity for God to speak to us through His Word, through others, and through the prayers we share.

So often we can get caught up in looking for God's big directions to come. But perhaps it's the day-to-day discipline of seeking God that prepares us for whatever God has in store for us. Clearly, this was true for Mary. Even though she had been visited by an angel, she continued to practice her Jewish faith and to do things that were required of every faithful person. She did not wait for more supernatural appearances. Instead, she sought God in a way that we can easily emulate: She went to a house of worship.

What she heard there was disconcerting. The promise of a sword that would pierce her soul is not the sort of prediction any mother wants to hear in regard to her child. God began preparing Mary, from the earliest days of her motherhood, for all that she would have to face. And in one way or another, virtually every parent experiences difficult times with the children they love. The "sword" may come in the form of rebellion, drug use, or the abandonment of our lifestyle or values. And yet even when those things happen, God can still be present in our lives. He alone can strengthen us to face troubling circumstances, and He knows best how to guide us through them. Joseph and Mary had to practice perseverance in the unique parenting task to which they were called, and with God's help, we too can persevere through every parenting challenge that comes our way.

In my life, one of the most difficult challenges I faced as a mother occurred in the early 1980s. One of our daughters became anorexic, and at times her life was in danger. I had prayed every prayer I knew how to pray—spoken every word of love and encouragement I could muster. It seemed as if nothing could touch the depth of self-rejection that drove her. Finally, I came to a point at which I prayed this painful prayer: "Father, I know that her behavior could kill her, and I release her to you. I ask you to care for her as a loving Father—but I release her to you." It was a prayer that cost me many tears and much pain.

I know many other Christian parents have prayed in this way for their hurting children and never see the turn-around their hearts desire. I do not know why God chose to give me the desire of my heart and slowly turn our daughter away from her self-destructive path. Today, she is a healthy young woman. We are no more deserving or spiritual than other parents who pray with aching hearts—with souls that feel as if a sword has been run through them.

Yes, we may seek comfort and counsel from others—but fear and hurt can drive us into the arms of God, our heavenly confidant, as almost no other impulses can. We so enjoy the company of others—but how do we cultivate the company and confidential friendship of God?

I suggest we look to Mary's example and the price she paid. Psalms 141:3 gives us the wisdom Mary seems to have grasped: "Set a guard over my mouth, O Lord; keep watch over the door of my lips."

In discussing Mary's gentle, intriguing silence, the French author Jean Guitton notes that perhaps "she understood that where divinity is at work the initiatives must be left to God."[2]

How often do we charge prayerlessly into situations with our futile human efforts and disrupt God's initiatives? Scripture witnesses Mary restraining herself from inter-fering in God's sovereign business. She let God speak for himself to Joseph, and then she obeyed the guidance Joseph received (Matthew 1:18–25; 2:13–23). She treasured the precious moments of awe and wonder, and patiently pon-dered the moments of foreboding as well (Luke 2:19, 33).

The way in which Joseph and Mary each accepted their

role can also speak to us about the cost of making family work. The grace Joseph displayed, accepting the cost of responsibility to raise Jesus as his own son, is a testimony to true masculine strength—strength that does not rely on physical might or ego. Joseph readily adopted Jesus as his legal son and heir, which was accomplished by his presentation of Jesus at the temple. This reflects, in an earthly way, each believer's adoption by God.

And there is another significance to Joseph's adoption of Jesus: Through Joseph's lineage as well as through Mary's, God prepared the birth of His Son down to the last detail, providing Jesus with impeccable credentials as the Anointed One. Both Luke and Matthew provide genealogies of Jesus. According to scholars, Luke traces Jesus' genealogy to Adam, the first man, while Matthew goes back to the father of the Hebrew people, Abraham.

The *MacArthur New Testament Commentary* explains the importance of these family histories:

> Matthew's intent is to validate Jesus' royal claim by showing His legal descent from David through Joseph, who was Jesus' legal, though not natural, father. Luke's intent is to trace Jesus' actual royal blood ancestry through his mother, thereby establishing His racial lineage from David. Matthew follows the royal line through David and Solomon, David's son and successor to the throne. Luke follows the royal line through Nathan, another son of David. Jesus was therefore the blood descendant of David through Mary, and the legal descendant of David through Joseph. Genealogically, Jesus was perfectly qualified to take the throne of David.[3]

Matthew's genealogy includes four women, all former outcasts. They are, in fact, the only women listed until

Mary is mentioned. The four women included in that list are all examples of God's grace.

The first was Tamar, Judah's Canaanite daughter-in-law who was involved in prostitution. The second outcast was a gentile as well—Rahab of Jericho, who protected Israel's spies. God spared her and her family and brought her into the Messianic line as the wife of Salmon and mother of Boaz, David's great-grandfather. Then there is Ruth, the gentile wife of Boaz, who was grandmother to King David. The last woman included is Bathsheba, mentioned as the wife of David and former wife of Uriah. David had an affair with her and had her husband killed in battle. As David's wife she became the mother of Solomon.

When I see these women included in the line of succession to Jesus, I am reminded how God gives His grace to sinners who turn to Him. Because He numbered sinners among His *forebears*, it should be no surprise that Jesus asks them, also by grace, to be His *heirs*. And we may become His own when we count the cost—as many did— and follow Him.

It comes down to choices, the great and the small ones. Yes, we can choose our own way and strive with our human might to "be all that we can be." But that is not the path of salvation. Instead, we are asked to let God make us all that *He* desires. When we pay the price to follow God's way, we find that He does not waste us; rather, He invests us as gold.

Mary seems to have embodied a favorite passage of Scripture: Psalm 25:4–5 says, "Show me your ways, O Lord, teach me your paths; guide me in your truth and teach me, for you are God my Savior, and my hope is in you all day long."

Every one of us can pray this psalm, even as Mary might have prayed it. No matter how challenging our path, God will gift us with grace and strength if we willingly give our hearts to Him.

Questions to Ponder

1. Are worship, prayer, and Bible study part of my daily discipline? How may I be more faithful to God in these things?
2. How have I sensed God's preparation in my life; and how have I seen it in the past? Have I reached the point in my walk with Christ where I can affirm my faith even at times when it seems a sword is piercing my very soul?
3. What are the things I need to keep to myself and discuss only with God? Can I be trusted with the confidences of my children, my spouse, and others?

*A*n angel of the Lord appeared to Joseph in a dream. "Get up," he said, "take the child and his mother and escape to Egypt. Stay there until I tell you, for Herod is going to search for the child to kill him."

So he got up, took the child and his mother during the night and left for Egypt, where he stayed until the death of Herod. And so was fulfilled what the Lord had said through the prophet: "Out of Egypt I called my son."

When Herod realized that he had been outwitted by the Magi, he was furious, and he gave orders to kill all the boys in Bethlehem and its vicinity who were two years old and under, in accordance with the time he had learned from the Magi. Then what was said through the prophet Jeremiah was fulfilled:

"A voice is heard in Ramah,
weeping and great mourning,
Rachel weeping for her children
and refusing to be comforted,
because they are no more."

After Herod died, an angel of the Lord appeared in a dream to Joseph in Egypt and said, "Get up, take the child and his mother and go to the land of Israel, for those who were trying to take the child's life are dead."

So he got up, took the child and his mother and went to the land of Israel. . . . And he went and lived in a town called Nazareth. So was fulfilled what was said through the prophets: "He will be called a Nazarene."

MATTHEW 2:13–23

6

Courage to Follow

FOR SOME REASON, an elderly man chose us from among the numerous tourists and secretly motioned us to follow him to the back of the Basilica of the Nativity. He used a huge metal key to open a heavy gate and led us down a dark, ancient stairwell.

Our tour guide, a Christian friend who lived in Israel, had led many tours through the church. "But I've never seen anyone allowed to use these stairs," she said.

Our elderly friend led us down a tunnel. On one side we passed a door that opened to the spot marked as the place of the original manger in which Jesus lay. The tunnel we were now traveling in was the back of the manger cave, according to the guide.

The old man led us in the direction of a newly exposed cave—or so he explained in broken English. The pitch of his voice rose excitedly as he told my tour-guide friend about this site. In this cave, recent excavations had unearthed the bones of babies and very young children. They were believed to be the remains of the little boys slain by Herod when he sought to kill the infant Jesus.

Staring into the dark stone cavern, my eyes slowly adjusted to the dim light. I tried to imagine the terror Mary would have felt, learning that the king himself wanted to take the life of her son. What fear must have tried to grip her when Joseph awakened her for their night time escape to Egypt.

Herod was an Edomite usurper, who had no right to rule the Jews. He was placed on the throne by Rome, and protected by this foreign military force. Herod feared the Magi's declaration about a newborn king.

Since he was not Jewish, Herod married a Hebrew woman to make himself more acceptable to the Jews he governed. A good politician, Herod used every trick he could devise to endear himself to the people. He was, however, a ruthless and paranoid figure. Fearing a threat to his power, he had the high priest, who was his wife's brother, drowned. Then he had his wife killed, followed by her mother and two of his own sons. Five days before his own death he ordered that a third son be executed.

One scholar tells of even more bizarre behavior:

> One of the greatest evidences of [Herod's] bloodthirstiness and insane cruelty was having the most distinguished citizens of Jerusalem arrested and imprisoned shortly before his death. Because he knew no one would mourn his own death, he gave orders for those prisoners to be executed the moment he died—in order to guarantee that there would be mourning in Jerusalem.[1]

Herod ordered his sister and brother-in-law to execute the prisoners. Fearing the Jews' wrath, though, they freed them in Herod's name before news of his death became known. Understanding Herod's demented character helps to explain his abhorrent order to execute every boy under two years old in Bethlehem and the surrounding territory.

It was the Magi who inadvertently alerted Herod to Jesus' birth. Then, through a dream, God told them to leave Israel without reporting back to Herod the identity of the infant king. Feeling he had been tricked, Herod was furious and frightened. But why did he have every boy under two years of age killed?

First, we are not certain how long after Jesus' birth the Magi arrived in Jerusalem. Quite likely, Herod was uncertain how long before their arrival the star had appeared. Had it appeared before the actual birth—and if so, how long before? After all, the Magi had come a great distance. Because of these uncertainties, Herod's sick and diabolical personality apparently triggered his plan to execute the Christ-child.

No one knows for sure when the Magi came, or exactly who they were, though legends have developed that identify them by name. God, in His own way, guided those wealthy and knowledgeable men to seek the virgin-born child. We do know that these sages of the East were humbled in His presence and bowed before Him. It was an Eastern custom to pay homage to a king with gifts, and they brought treasures befitting a king: gold, possibly in the form of gold dust; frankincense, a fragrant resin from eastern Africa; and myrrh, a rare, orange-colored gum used as a perfume.

Looking at the scriptural account of the unexpected flight of Mary, Joseph, and Jesus, we see a practical use for the Magi's gifts: An ever-watchful God may have used these gifts to provide for their trip and support them in Egypt. Joseph and Mary endured untold dangers as they fled. Desolation marked their way over Beersheba's hills and through Sinai's barren desert. They would need to remain alert, watching for bands of marauders.

Some scholars believe their flight occurred approximately one year after Jesus' birth, so it is possible that the young family spent the better part of a year in Egypt. As their time of hiding came to a close, God spoke to Joseph again, confirming that Joseph was God's ordained caretaker for Jesus and Mary.

When Joseph, Mary, and Jesus returned from Egypt, they originally headed back toward Bethlehem, but God redirected them to Nazareth. Perhaps their plan was to settle in Bethlehem, thus avoiding the gossip in Nazareth about Mary's pregnancy. But in sheer obedience, those three seasoned travelers of great destiny returned to Mary's hometown. Mary and Joseph must have had plenty of time to think as they endured yet another arduous journey. Not knowing what the days ahead would hold, they traveled on, holding only to each other and to their faith in the God of Israel.

Fear and Faith

Three strangely dressed men from the East walked away from the small dwelling in Bethlehem, where Mary watched from an open doorway. She looked up the hill to see if any villagers were still watching, curious about the unusual guests. A sense of wonder lingered in the humble home as the young mother fingered the royal gifts the men had given her son.

Mary was deep in revery about the Magi. *They were so sure they would find a special child—a child of destiny. They risked so much, traveled so far to see my little one. Once again, my God, you have given witness to the awesome plan you must have for Him. But what will it mean?*

It had not escaped Joseph's wise notice that the Magi were gentiles. He had remarked, "Isn't it strange? Whatever Jesus has been selected to accomplish for God must extend beyond our own people."

That night, Mary settled on her bed, with the newborn breathing rhythmically close to her side. One tiny hand strayed from the covers and touched her cheek. She began to drift into a sleep that was wrapped in a deep contentment. . . .

And then someone gently shook her by the shoulders. She startled awake, looking up into Joseph's face. In the dim light—she could detect a look of concern. "What's the matter?" she asked, immediately roused.

"I had another dream—one of the dreams from God," he said. "Jesus is in danger here. We need to leave and go to Egypt. Now."

Mary sat up and steadied herself. "Egypt—are you sure? That will take days."

Joseph went outside and led their donkey up to the doorway. Mary packed food and clothes, feeling caught in a great tide of events. With a growing feeling of anxiety in the pit of her stomach, Mary carried items outside to him, and Joseph tucked them hurriedly into packs laid over the donkey's back. Carefully, he stowed the gifts of the Magi. Joseph whispered to her, "Those valuables will see us through for a long time." Finally, Mary came out carrying the still-sleeping Jesus.

Joseph held the infant in his arms as Mary mounted

the donkey. Then he handed Jesus back to her.

Quietly, in haste, the family slipped unseen from the village as the first blushes of light tinted the rocky hills. Joseph was careful even to avoid the shepherds' fields. No one witnessed their leaving.

The journey took them through the barren Sinai and taxed all of Mary's skills as a new mother. They could not travel under the burning sun, and Mary had the challenges, in this wilderness, of keeping Jesus clean and fed and well-rested. When He cried, her heart would skip with fear of being overheard by another traveler, who might carry news back to Herod's soldiers of their flight. She did her best to stay calm for the sake of her little one.

In Egypt, they found there were other Israelite refugee families—families who had fled from the demented actions of Herod for all sorts of reasons. But they were all refugees, nonetheless, not especially welcomed by the Egyptians. Joseph found work and kept to his daily prayers. Even so, they felt like strangers in a foreign land.

And then, traders brought news of the horror in Bethlehem. Herod's soldiers had stormed into every household in Bethlehem. Swords in hand, they raged from house to house, searching for little boys under two years of age. Each time they saw a baby, they ripped its clothing off to see what sex it was. The boys were killed—murdered right before their parents' eyes. Many men were killed also, trying to save their sons.

Mary felt as if her heart were pierced—she could hear in her mind the high lamenting wail of the grieving women. For days she fasted the fast of the mourning. Joseph moved silently, grimly through his days. . . .

And then one night, Joseph again had a dream. He was instructed to return to Israel with Mary and Jesus. The next morning he prepared their donkey for the journey. What would await them on the last leg of this heaven-directed journey, Mary could only wonder. The donkey swayed beneath her, its short, chopping stride creating a familiar rhythm as it plodded homeward. Absently, she kissed her sleepy-eyed boy on the forehead. *Thank you for keeping Him safe, Lord.*

You must be our refuge, she mused, half in thought, half in prayer, *for we have no other. Isn't that what you have taught our people? I must never forget. You have been faithful to us always. I have to trust in that.*

Joseph became concerned for Mary on the third day when, in her grief for the bereaved mothers of Bethlehem, she still would not eat. Finally, he coaxed her to take nourishment "for the boy—he's nursing, and a healthy eater."

Other travelers on the road excitedly told them more recent news from Israel. Herod had died, his stomach eaten by worms. Herod's son Archelaus reigned now, and he was no less a madman. Joseph shifted uneasily at this news. That night, in another dream, he was directed to take the family back to Nazareth. "It is much too dangerous in Bethlehem," he told Mary in the morning.

Mary felt a mix of unsettling emotions at this. She would get to go home after all—back to the town where she had been raised, where all her relatives and the friends of her girlhood lived. She was eager to see them all—but how would they treat her and her family? Would they see her as a sinful woman who became pregnant before marriage? Or would they recognize her son for who He was? Would life ever be ordinary again?

Still, these hill-country people were *her* people—and Jesus' people, too. Step by step they went back to Nazareth, facing a future Mary anticipated . . . and feared. She didn't know what their future held, but her trust was in God, who held their future.

Courage and Commitment

God still draws both the humble and the high-born, the rich and the poor, to His Son—for to Him our ways of measuring worth and status mean nothing. The truth is that we "all have sinned and fall short of the glory of God" (Romans 3:23). And Jesus will receive all who come to worship Him. We are "justified freely by his grace through the redemption that came by Christ Jesus" (Romans 3:24).

Imagine Mary's awe when she saw the Magi bow to worship her son. It was another opening of the hand of heaven as it reached into their everyday lives. The way in which God presents gifts to us may be far less dramatic, yet I believe His hand is evident in our lives today, if only we will look for it. Our human nature quickly forgets God's touches. Sometimes we forget His greatest blessings, and our attitude says, "What have you done for me lately?"

Mary must have had so many questions as she and Joseph fled to Egypt, fearing for Jesus' very life. Questions may have surged in her as they returned to Nazareth. Yet Scripture gives us no hint that Mary thought of her own comfort; she and Joseph did not feel God owed them anything. Just the opposite appears to be true: They continued to owe God their willing obedience to do as He commanded, even when they were forced to take risks and experience extreme personal inconvenience.

Mary's example is a great encouragement to me, because the Bible promises that the steadfastness God gave to her is available to all believers. Mary drew strength from the God whose plan she sought to follow. She must have learned, as she yielded herself to Him, that He alone was responsible for her.

There is no greater strength. When we receive Christ and His salvation, committing our lives to Him, we enter into a *covenant*—an agreement of honor with God. As we seek Him and His plan, He takes responsibility for us. Just as He proved to Mary, God does not break His promise.

You may feel that God has called you to a task. Perhaps He has opened opportunities for you, yet you don't feel equipped to meet the challenge. The example of Mary and Joseph teaches a central biblical truth: If God calls you to a task, He will equip you to do it. He takes responsibility for us! As a wise friend says, "God doesn't call the equipped—He equips the called."

Consider the magnitude of the events that occurred in the life of young Mary in just the two years following her visit from the angel Gabriel. Her entire world turned upside-down. Her life careened from one exciting or frightening event to another, in rapid succession: the question of her marriage to Joseph, the arduous trek to Bethlehem in her last days of pregnancy, her child's birth in a stable, the shepherds' amazing story, the visit of rich and powerful men from the East, the bittersweet prophecy in the temple, the night flight through the desert, Herod's slaughter of innocent babies, the time spent as aliens in Egypt, and their desert trek home.

It all seems more than one young woman could handle. If Mary began as a weak, retiring female, she was transformed into anything but that! I suspect that God already knew her mettle, and that He ordered the events of her life to reveal a valiant human being. Since God created women to be mothers and nurturers, He equipped us with great sensitivity. We are relational and caring by nature. We communicate love easily, and we feel deeply.

But a great strength can become a great weakness when overplayed. Our feelings can lie. They can be capricious and far from dependable. Only God is unchanging. Have we learned yet that He is the only reliable element in our fast-changing world? Even in the midst of hard circumstances that we do not understand, and even when we fail Him—at all times we can trust in God's unchanging love. When everything and everyone fails us, we can rest in the fact that God's love for us has not changed. When we fix our souls on this foundational truth, we open a new door through which God steps into our lives to give grace.

Of all people who were privileged with the very presence of God in their lives, Mary and Joseph could surely have laid claim to special favors from God. Yet they continued to live in meager circumstances, and they faced unimaginable dangers without bitterness. And through it all, God remained faithful to them, giving them inner grace to survive. Truly, the kingdom of God had begun to unfold in their lives.

Do we, as believers, sometimes hold wrong expectations toward God? A life committed to God is not a life of automatic ease and comfort. God did not even provide this to the mother of His Son and the earthly father who raised Him. As we grow in our understanding of what God wants us to do with our lives, the challenges may very well increase. Yet there is surely no greater privilege than living a Christ-centered life—no matter what the cost in earthly terms.

To me, one of the most compelling contemporary examples of this principle is Mother Teresa. I was once privileged to spent time during a luncheon with this diminutive woman in the Senate Caucus Room in Washington, D.C. With its high ceilings, chandeliers, and lavish marble, the room is big and impressive. Mother Teresa entered the room, appearing even smaller than I'd anticipated. She looked so little, and she was dressed in a simple blue and white habit, beat-up old sandals, and a moth-eaten gray sweater, which she would also wear to the White House for a reception the next day.

As she took her place, everyone stood and applauded with tears in their eyes. I watched in wonder, and thought, *Lord, this woman possesses more power than I see walking in the halls of Congress. She doesn't own anything, she doesn't shake her fist and demand her rights, and she never asks for anything for herself. In obedience to you, she has reached down into the gutter and loved those the world considers unlovable. She is a bundle of walking love—and that is her power.*

To me, Mother Teresa embodies an eternal perspective: She takes no thought for herself. On another occasion, a friend of mine led Mother Teresa on a tour of the White House. As they passed the state dining room, Mother Teresa observed, "They have a lot of big dinners here." My friend agreed, fully expecting Mother Teresa to ask, as do so many people, if she could be invited to a state dinner. And it caught my friend off-guard when the little woman at her side asked, "What do they do with all the leftover food?" She was wondering, of course, if these elegant cast-offs found their way to the poor.

I imagine that Mother Teresa views life from a perspective in which each individual is valued. Perhaps her outlook can help us come to grips with one of the most difficult parts of this narrative: Herod's slaughter of the innocents. How can we begin to understand the cost exacted from the women who lost little boys during the massacre in Bethlehem? Yet at the same time, is this really so foreign to our experience? I often grieve over the 1.5 million abortions performed in America alone each year—to me, a contemporary slaughter of the innocents.

I believe this gruesome episode contains wisdom for today. Those babies torn from their mothers' arms were not quickly forgotten. And babies torn from their mothers' wombs are not quickly torn from their hearts; grief for those lost children is long-enduring. Their mourning sometimes is latent, yet pastors and counselors know the buried sorrow and pain will surface sometime in some way. The reality of post-abortion trauma is kept out of sight and out of mind as some seek to preserve abortion-on-demand. Yet every life is precious to God who created man and woman in His image, giving us intrinsic value even at conception.

Judged by contemporary logic-of-convenience, Mary's out-of-wedlock pregnancy, with its personal danger and obvious emotional trauma, would have made Jesus a prime candidate for abortion today. Perhaps Mary's determined commitment offers an example—a challenge for us to continue in our efforts to protect today's unborn innocents, who are being sacrificed on the altar of selfishness and convenience. Can healing come to a land that permits the slaughter of innocent babies and inflicts emotional violence on the souls of their mothers? Whom can the Lord count on today to oppose this evil? Today, God is still looking for those who will be faithful in small tasks, knowing that He can trust them with even greater things.

Have you sensed a far-reaching call, like Mary, like Joseph? On this we can rely: If we answer His call, God will accomplish mighty things through us, with an unending supply of grace for the long, hard road.

Questions to Ponder

[handwritten: my family, parents, sisted, brothes, friends]

1. What gifts has God given to bless you and provide for you? Who are the "Magi" in your life—the people God has used to convey His gifts and blessings to you?
2. What are the difficulties you face as you seek to carry out God's plan for your life? What is the "Egypt"—the hard or unfamiliar circumstance—He might be calling you toward? How might the response of Mary and Joseph shape your own response to God?
3. If you believe abortion is a modern-day "slaughter of the innocents," what could you do to help counter its effects? Have you considered volunteering at a crisis pregnancy center; marching for life; writing letters to your elected officials or to newspapers?

*E*very year [Jesus'] parents went to Jerusalem for the Feast of the Passover. When he was twelve years old, they went up to the Feast, according to the custom. After the Feast was over, while his parents were returning home, the boy Jesus stayed behind in Jerusalem, but they were unaware of it. Thinking he was in their company, they traveled on for a day. Then they began looking for him among their relatives and friends.

When they did not find him, they went back to Jerusalem to look for him. After three days they found him in the temple courts, sitting among the teachers, listening to them and asking them questions. Everyone who heard him was amazed at his understanding and his answers.

When his parents saw him, they were astonished. His mother said to him, "Son, why have you treated us like this? Your father and I have been anxiously searching for you."

"Why were you searching for me?" he asked. "Didn't you know I had to be in my Father's house?" But they did not understand what he was saying to them.

Then he went down to Nazareth with them and was obedient to them. But his mother treasured all these things in her heart. And Jesus grew in wisdom and stature, and in favor with God and men.

LUKE 2:41–52

1. intellectually – mind (mentally)
2. physically
3. spiritually
4. socially

7

Into God's Hands

THE BIBLE IS SILENT about the lives of Jesus, Mary, and Joseph from the time they return from Egypt until Jesus began His public ministry at about the age of thirty—with one exception.

The Gospel of Luke tells of an incident that occurred when Jesus, at age twelve, stood at the threshold of maturity. At this pivotal point in His development, Jesus caused considerable anguish for His parents by remaining in Jerusalem after the Passover feast. But it is also the first time we hear Him articulating an understanding of His own relationship to God the Father, the first time we see Him decisively stepping apart from his family and from the religious and political leaders.

Any parent with a preadolescent child can surely relate to the strong mixed emotions Mary must have felt when she discovered Jesus was not where she thought He was. What did she feel as she looked for Him for those three days? Or when she finally found Him, safe and going about the activities to which God had called Him?

To set the stage for this event—which reveals so much about the Lord's earthly family and heavenly calling—we must consider the Passover. In many ways, this feast was the centerpiece of the Jewish calendar and occurred annually in the spring. It marked the protection God provided the Jewish people during their exile in Egypt and celebrated their deliverance from slavery.

In New Testament times, Passover was an occasion for whole families to travel to Jerusalem from all over Israel. As many as 100,000 visitors would crowd the city, which ordinarily held about 25,000 people.[1] Tradition called for the sacrifice of a pure, unblemished lamb, commemorating God's instructions to Moses. Each Hebrew household in exile was to kill a lamb, use its blood to mark the doorframe, and eat the roasted meat (Exodus 12:3–11). Then the Lord "passed over" those houses sprinkled with the blood of the lamb and spared their firstborn children and animals, while He brought judgment on the people of Egypt. The celebration of Passover held deep spiritual and national significance:

> *Passover* was and is the festival of freedom and redemption par excellence. Representative of God's love and saving acts, it always gave the people hope in the face of physical and spiritual oppression. As a family celebration, it served as a unifying bond from generation to generation. Its strength is seen in its emergence as the most important of Jewish festivals, in its three-thousand-year continuity, and in its continuing relevance to the needs of the people. . . .[2]

Only the men were required to go to Jerusalem to observe Passover, yet Luke records that both Mary and Joseph went there every year. To me this is further evidence that Mary revered God's Word as part of her everyday life, and it suggests that she played an active role in Jesus' spiritual training at home.

Alfred Edersheim, the great historian, singles out Mary's impact on her son:

> The influence exerted upon His early education, especially by His mother, seems implied throughout the gospel history. Of course, His was a pious Jewish home; and at Nazareth there was a synagogue, to which . . . a school was probably attached. . . . But, whether or not Jesus had attended such a school, His mind was so thoroughly imbued with the Sacred Scriptures—He was so familiar with them in their every detail—that we cannot fail to infer that the home of Nazareth possessed a precious copy of its own of the entire Sacred Volume, which from earliest childhood formed, so to speak, the meat and drink of the God-Man.[3]

It was one thing for Mary and Joseph to train their son conscientiously in the practice of their faith; it was quite another to see and hear Jesus suddenly come of age spiritually. When they found Him in the temple, perhaps they expected a contrite confession that he had not been where he was supposed to be. Mary's first words to her "lost" son will resonate with every mother who has found herself in similar circumstances: "Son, why have you treated us like this?"

Yet Jesus offers no apology. Instead of answering His mother, Jesus questions her: "Why were you searching for me? Didn't you know I had to be in my Father's house?"

To call God "my Father" was a new way for a Jew to speak. In the Old Testament, this sort of personalization of God occurs only prophetically. When God spoke to the prophet Nathan, this personal relationship was referenced: "I will be his father, and he will be my son" (2 Samuel 7:14). That prophecy referred to the coming Messiah. And in Psalm 89:26 the Father says, speaking of the one who would hold a singular claim to sonship, "He will call out to me, 'You are my Father. . . .'"

When Jesus said "My Father's house," therefore, He hinted at the as-yet-unrevealed role He would play in purchasing the salvation of the world. We must recognize the significance that rests in the fact that Jesus revealed this aspect of His true nature at the time of the Passover—for He was to become our sacrificial lamb, our God-given, once-and-for-all deliverance from bondage to sin.

The incident in the temple must have left an indelible impression on Mary. It drew an invisible line between Jesus and His earthly parents. For Mary and Joseph, it marked the beginning of the long and painful process every parent goes through: the process of letting go.

Missing

The Passover feast had ended, and a caravan of travelers from Nazareth prepared to return home from Jerusalem. Getting the animals assembled and the packs loaded was an especially difficult chore for parents with very young children. How well Mary remembered past trips to crowded Jerusalem to observe Passover! It was a constant challenge to get organized while Jesus ran about with the other boys, dashing in front of donkeys and hiding behind bundles being readied for the trip home. Now that Jesus was twelve, He could be off by himself. Mary silently thanked God for the good, responsible boy He had given her.

She checked with Joseph to make sure he had everything he needed for the trip home; then she went back to where the women and children were preparing to leave. She swept her cousin's two little boys up into her arms, remembering how precious Jesus was at their age. "I'll take care of these little mischief-makers," she told her cousin. "You finish getting ready."

As was the custom, the women and young children traveled at the front of the caravan, while the men, older boys, and donkeys followed. When it was time to begin the homeward trek, Mary was deep in conversation with her cousin, offering encouragement about child rearing. Walking down the steep hillsides from Jerusalem, and over the Kidron brook, Mary was absorbed in talk and never gave Jesus' whereabouts a second thought. He had grown so tall and mature over the past year that Mary simply envisioned Him among the men—perhaps with Joseph.

When the travelers stopped for the night, each family gathered to eat and sleep together. Mary and Joseph found a spot to spread out their things, and Mary set out food for their meal. "This night is warm for the season," Joseph remarked as he covered his head to begin the evening prayers.

After prayers, as they prepared to sit down to their meal, Mary realized she had not seen Jesus even once all day. She studied the campsites of their fellow Nazarenes and looked out toward the horizon. Jesus often went walking by himself—but surely he would want to have dinner. "Did you tell Jesus to meet us for dinner?" she asked Joseph.

Joseph looked up at her quizzically. "I haven't told Him

anything. I thought He spent the day with you."

A shock of dread touched Mary's whole being.

Abandoning their meal, Joseph and Mary set out to find Him. "Some of the older boys are over there," Joseph said, gesturing to a hillside where a group was playing among twisted olive trees. "I will ask them, and you ask the others."

Mary went to each family in turn to learn whether they had seen her son. One woman could not resist a jibe—especially since Jesus never seemed to do anything wrong. "Now you know what it's like to see your boy turn into a man. I haven't been able to keep track of my son for a day since he turned thirteen."

Mary kept on searching, ignoring the stray comments. Still, no Jesus. As dusk darkened into nightfall, she searched the hills one last time, then came back to their site. Joseph was there already, his face grim. "There is nowhere else to look," he said.

The other families were settling down for the night, and Mary's cousin came over. "Have you found Jesus?" she asked. Mary could only shake her head in reply. Her cousin hugged her reassuringly, while Mary fought silently against the fear welling up inside.

Long into the night, Joseph and Mary sat by the fire, alert, as if their very vigilance would draw Jesus back. Perhaps each felt a natural guilt and helpless frustration. *Why didn't we check on Him before we left? How could we have left Him behind?* In the darkness, that raw fear they had known during their flight to Egypt tried to wrap itself around them again.

When the new day dawned, Mary started out of a fitful half-sleep. "What are we going to do?" she asked Joseph, who was already up and stirring the fire to life. The other families readied themselves to continue heading homeward.

"We have to go back to Jerusalem. Jesus must still be there."

The day dragged on intolerably, and the sun beat on their backs as they returned to the city. Each prayed fervently. Each time they passed a caravan of travelers heading north toward Galilee, they asked after their son. And each time the answer was no.

When Mary and Joseph entered Jerusalem's gates that evening, it was nearly dark, and they needed to find a room, eat, and try once again to sleep. Through the night, Mary continued to wake with a start. *O God*, she prayed, *forgive me for being so negligent.*

In the morning, they made their way through the crowded marketplace—Jesus was not in sight—then along the narrow streets leading up to the open courtyard before the temple. As they entered among the temple's tall pillars, they found a group of religious teachers seated together, their eyes focused in rapt attention on someone. And then they saw—in relief and irritation—their missing son.

Men three and four times Jesus' age surrounded Him. Calmly, Jesus looked up as Mary rushed forward, while Joseph folded his arms sternly. The religious leaders smiled as Jesus' mother broke the silence: "Son, why have you treated us like this? Your father and I have been searching all over for you!"

"Why were you *searching* for me?" Jesus rejoined her. "Didn't you know I had to be in my Father's house?"

Too relieved to be angry, Mary didn't pursue the remarks. Joseph, feeling unkempt from travel and dreadfully provincial next to these urbane scholars, signaled that He should come immediately. Without another word, Jesus obediently followed his earthly father out of the temple. The three of them journeyed back to Nazareth, and Jesus continued to live in quiet obedience to Mary and Joseph.

Mary would memorize each detail of what had happened that Passover week. Once more she stored Jesus' unusual words deep in her heart, reflecting on what they might mean. "Oh, God, in some ways Jesus is just a boy— but in other ways He's already so much more. He's like the boys He plays with, and at the same time so different. We teach Him about you and your law. He listens and He learns, yet He seems somehow to know already."

Mary was approaching thirty at this time, and her face reflected her many trying experiences and emotions. She had lost none of the warmth from her smile, but now her eyes spoke of an inner depth borne of experience. For long years, their life in Nazareth had been so quiet—so ordinary. Why did this incident so disquiet her? It was as if a season of life were passing. Change was coming; she could feel it. And her obedient son was beginning to act according to another voice that had greater claim on His allegiance. For now, He would tuck himself back into the role of carpenter's son—but one day, He would walk out the door of their home, as all grown children must. How would Mary respond when the moment came?

Family Ties

As a wife and mother, Mary usually led an ordinary life. Even on the annual pilgrimage to Jerusalem, she was obliged to do many mundane, ordinary things: caring for her family, helping others with child care. No doubt she was faithful in little things, doing them "as unto the Lord." Similarly, each of us has a list of ordinary tasks we must perform every day. And, like Mary, we often need to be reawakened to God's greater plans. Once again, eternity had to interrupt Mary's life and she had to choose: either to open herself to a deeper awareness of Jesus' identity, or to reject His shifting allegiance.

How many of us, in the midst of doing all the things we need to do, are plagued by the feeling that perhaps we are "missing the boat?" Wouldn't God be much happier with us if we could *do* more? Serve Him on a mission field? Or compose beautiful music? Or have more time to help with projects at church? Do we get so caught up in ourselves and our tasks that we are in danger of missing an important bend in the path?

Eternity *will* interrupt time. As we await God's presence and direction in the midst of the mundane, it helps to take Mary's experience to heart. We, too, need reminders of Jesus' identity. We can fix our hearts on the fact of His divine identity and mission, which He announced to Mary and Joseph in the temple.

How does God come to us today, in the midst of our routine days and homely tasks?

Those of us who are mothers often feel that the most tiresome and meaningless tasks of all are the ones involving child rearing: We lose sight of our purpose so easily in the endless changing of diapers, correcting the same misbehavior over and over, teaching little ones to share, guiding and directing children in the ups and downs of relationships, schooling, and sports. . . . It is crucial for every parent to step back and focus, from time to time, on the goal of parenting. This is essentially what had to happen for Mary in this story. She was, understandably, caught up in the moment—the fear of losing her son and the mixed anger and relief when they found Him again. Jesus pointed Mary toward her true final goal: to care for

Him and prepare Him—and ultimately to release Him into God's hands.

Similarly, we can remain sensitive and responsive to God's call on the lives of our children. In doing so we can begin to see the value and purpose even in the minor details of putting on a bandage, reading a bedtime story, remembering grace at mealtimes, or listening with undivided attention when a child comes to us needing to talk.

I believe motherhood is one of God's most effective and intensive spiritual training schools. It offers an unmatched opportunity to develop godly character. Yes, we have the task and privilege of teaching our children obedience, industry, perseverance, self-control—but there will always come a time when we will have to suffer separation. And when it is time to launch them out into the world, what a great sense of joy and deep satisfaction can be ours if we have sharpened our focus on God's plan for a child's life and not our own.

We cannot leave this brief episode without a look at the other influence in Jesus' young life—Joseph.

A father's involvement in child rearing can make a significant difference as a child prepares to launch out into the world. We know that Jesus learned from Joseph how to work with His hands. And most likely, after His father's death, He worked as a carpenter to support Mary before setting out on His public ministry. More important, however, was the spiritual role model Joseph provided. I believe that Jesus paid something of a compliment to Joseph when He referred to God in a personal way as "my Father." On what evidence do I base this?

True, there are only a few references to Joseph in the Bible, but from these we can glean a sense of what he must have been like as a father. It seems he was a man of unusual self-control, as we can see by his calm and compassionate response to the news that Mary was pregnant. His life was marked by a consistent sensitivity to God, who could speak to Joseph through dreams. As we have seen already, he observed the laws and customs of his Jewish faith. Perhaps it was at Joseph's knee that Jesus first uttered the word "Abba," or literally, "Daddy"—a term he later used to illustrate how every believer may experience a caring relationship with God. Perhaps Joseph's rough carpenter's hands patiently guided the hands of young Jesus as he eagerly sought to imitate Joseph's wood-working skills and creativity.

Some men sadly ignore or misuse the high position God has entrusted to them as the head of their families. This does not mean that a woman should view her biblical role in the family as inferior. Not in the least! Children need two healthy adult role models, and energy is sapped by fruitless jockeying for power and position. Just the opposite spirit appears to prevail in the marriage of Mary and Joseph. It would seem that their shared goal was to meet the challenge of raising a child with a destiny.

Do our children each have a destiny? Are we working in unity together for a purpose greater than ourselves—or pulling against one another?

Under the best circumstances, a godly home wraps a child in a blanket of security. It offers a safe haven from the world, a place where a child can let down his or her guard. And it is from this secure base that a child can be launched into healthy adulthood.

Jesus must have sensed those human feelings of security and unconditional acceptance in the home Joseph and Mary created. Secure in their love, as He was in His Father's love—He was prepared to step out into His public ministry. And in love His earthly parents had to keep in view God's plan, and learn how to guide their son with open hands.

Yes, Jesus would return to Nazareth with Mary and Joseph. But I suspect that, after this Passover incident, things were never quite the same.

Are you open and willing for eternity to step in and direct you and those you love toward change?

Questions to Ponder

1. What are the everyday tasks to which God has called me? What are the most important relationships in my life? Am I being attentive to these tasks and these relationships "as unto the Lord?"
2. What sort of family environment am I helping to create day by day? Is it one in which children can grow and thrive in peace and security?
3. How can I best prepare my children for the day when they will be out on their own? Will they know enough about God to relate to Him as their "Abba?"

*O*n the third day a wedding took place at Cana in Galilee. Jesus' mother was there, and Jesus and his disciples had also been invited to the wedding. When the wine was gone, Jesus' mother said to him, "They have no more wine."

"Dear woman, why do you involve me?" Jesus replied. "My time has not yet come."

His mother said to the servants, "Do whatever he tells you."

Nearby stood six stone water jars, the kind used by the Jews for ceremonial washing, each holding from twenty to thirty gallons. Jesus said to the servants, "Fill the jars with water"; so they filled them to the brim. Then he told them, "Now draw some out and take it to the master of the banquet."

They did so, and the master of the banquet tasted the water that had been turned into wine. . . . Then he called the bridegroom aside and said, "Everyone brings out the choice wine first and then the cheaper wine after the guests have had too much to drink; but you have saved the best till now."

This, the first of his miraculous signs, Jesus performed in Cana of Galilee. He thus revealed his glory, and his disciples put their faith in him. After this he went down to Capernaum with his mother and brothers and his disciples. . . .

JOHN 2:1–12

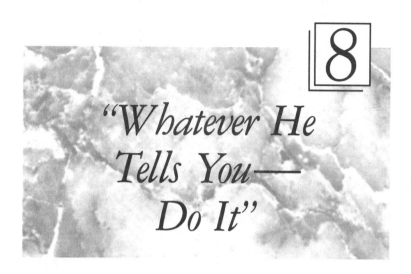

8

"Whatever He Tells You—Do It"

THE PICTURESQUE LITTLE VILLAGE of *Kafr Kanna* is presumed to be Cana of Galilee, the site of the wedding where Jesus performed His first recorded public miracle by changing water into wine.

It was a clear day when I visited the village church, a few miles north of Nazareth, purported to mark the site of that ancient wedding. It houses a well, said to be the one which provided water at the time. As we entered the village, I was amused by the creative, though somewhat irreverent, genius of a local merchant. Outside a cinder-block storefront was a homemade sign advertising "Fresh Jesus Wine."

Dust billowed around our car, and we had to avoid a

flock of bedraggled chickens that left a cloud of feathers flying as they ran. It made me consider one characteristic of Jesus and His ministry: He didn't choose the Palestinian equivalent of Carnegie Hall or the National Press Club as the site for His first miracle. In fact, it was accomplished in such a way that it did not draw attention to himself. Instead, it met a simple need for people He and Mary cared about. Looking into this incident raises a conflicting dynamic in Jesus and Mary's relationship: On one hand Jesus had a certain rapport with Mary as her son; on the other hand Mary had another kind of rapport with Jesus in the way a disciple must learn from a master.

Before we explore what happened at Cana, we must reconstruct exactly what was going on in the lives of Mary and Jesus at the time. To begin, Jesus was approaching age thirty and was still unmarried—a highly unusual circumstance for men of that time. Apparently He had continued to work quietly and unobtrusively as a carpenter, carrying on the trade He learned from Joseph.

Scripture is silent about the years between the incident in the temple, when Jesus was twelve, and the events that occurred just before the wedding at Cana. In Nazareth, we were given a rare opportunity to glimpse what life must have been like for Jesus and His family. An American missionary told us of a dig conducted directly under a Catholic convent about a block and a half from the Basilica of the Annunciation. The dig was not open for public viewing, he said, but the Mother Superior allowed him to come inside occasionally. When we were given permission to view the excavation and have a personal tour, we were delighted by the exciting discoveries coming to light.

The sisters had purchased the site from an elderly Arab woman, who told them it was reputed to be a holy site, though she did not know why. One morning after the nuns had acquired the property, their gardener was working in the courtyard and fell into what was presumed to be an old well. Subsequent digging, however, uncovered a tomb containing the skeletal remains of two men. Oddly, one was sitting upright and wearing a bishop's ring. Continued digging uncovered the pillars of a Byzantine-style church. Obviously they had discovered something significant, since the custom during the fifth century was to build churches over sites of Christian historical importance.

That hot day we followed our French guide, in tomb-like silence, to what remains a testimony to life long ago. We descended through dirt and rubble to what the nuns believe are the true remains of the home where Mary and Joseph lived. Because it cannot be proven, they make no claim. It is also a point of confusion and some disappointment for first-time visitors in Israel to find that almost every holy site has a rival. Archaeologists do attest that this particular site is indeed a first-century home, carved out of the hillside. Still intact are an arched door with a slot to insert a wooden bolt, and a small window. Across a narrow street-like path, steps lead down to the remains of an early well.

If this was their home, I wondered, *did Mary walk across this street to fill her buckets with water for her family? Did Jesus remove the bar on this door in the morning and prepare for a day's work?*

At some point when Jesus was a young man, Joseph apparently died, and eventually Jesus went off to live in Capernaum. In the week before the wedding feast at Cana, startling events overtook Galilee. John, the son of Elizabeth and Zechariah, had answered the call of God on his life and, according to Luke's Gospel, "went into all the country around the Jordan, preaching a baptism of repentance for the forgiveness of sins" (Luke 3:3). John attracted large crowds of people, who wondered if he might be the promised Messiah. John denied this vigorously.

When Jesus came to be baptized by John, marking the start of His ministry, John identified Him without hesitation: "_Look_—the Lamb of God, who takes away the sin of the world!" (John 1:29, emphasis added). And Jesus, after being baptized, began to draw His disciples from among the ordinary people of Galilee.

How much news about these events reached Mary in Nazareth? There is no way of knowing. Yet when she traveled to Cana for the wedding and met Jesus and His new disciples there, she clearly expected great things from Him.

Wedding feasts like the one at Cana often lasted seven days, during which wine flowed freely and poems and songs similar to those found in the Song of Solomon were performed in the couple's honor. The occasion marked a high point of social celebration, and no wedding host would stint on preparations for the festivities. This helps explain why running out of wine was such an embarrassment—a social _faux pas_ of the greatest magnitude.

Taken at face value, the miracle at Cana happened when Mary called her son's attention to a domestic dilemma. Jesus responded—but instead of addressing Mary as "mother" or by another obviously endearing term, Jesus said, "Woman, why do you involve me?" Some have interpreted this as harshness. That view is challenged by scholars who note that the correct translation reads, "Dear woman, what is that to you and me?" It was considered a gentle and endearing form of address, even though it may sound odd to us today. Basilea Schlink notes:

Jesus' answer to her, sometimes rendered as, "O

woman, what have you to do with me?" is usually misinterpreted. Literally it means, "What to me and to You?" (a Semitic formula), and does not have an unfriendly tone as it does in English.[1]

The exchange between Jesus and Mary resulted in a miracle, and the party continued even as the host praised the high quality of the new wine.

What is the spiritual significance of this first recorded miracle of Jesus? Is there a message in this seemingly unlikely choice for the Lord's first public miracle? Jesus taught the disciples that "the kingdom of heaven is like a king who prepared a wedding banquet for his son" (Matthew 22:2). And in Scripture, the redeemed believers are called the Bride of Christ, the Lamb of God, who was slain for the world's sins. Revelation 19 says, "Let us rejoice and be glad and give him glory! For the wedding of the Lamb has come, and his bride has made herself ready. . . . Blessed are those who are invited to the wedding supper of the Lamb." In Ephesians 5, Paul also compares the relationship between husband and wife to the relationship between Christ and the Church.

Here, then, is the significance: When Jesus changed water into wine at the wedding feast at Cana, the act was a sign pointing to the fact that He would provide wine for the guests at the wedding feast of the Lamb. Yes, there was great rejoicing at the marriage in Cana, but it was nothing compared to the coming celebration at the marriage of the Lamb.

But what of Mary? What motivated her? Did she understand God's timing? Had she heard that John the Baptist recognized her son and announced that Jesus was the Messiah? Did she realize His ministry had begun? Or did she have another reason? Consider Luci Shaw's suggestion:

Mary said yes to God. Did she wonder, during the next 30-odd years, why He had invaded her body and her life in such a shocking, unparalleled way, only to keep her waiting as her Son's years passed in the mundane dailyness of a small-town carpentry business? . . . Unfulfilled promise in a child is always painful for a human mother, especially when prolonged. Perhaps she needed the shocking first Announcement, those unforgettable memories, to keep her going, to rekindle her belief in his destiny.[2]

Mothers seem to have a special gift for remembering. Perhaps Mary was reflecting on how it all began three decades before. Perhaps she wondered now, "When will something happen with Jesus?" I believe that at Cana she sensed the time had come for her son to make known His true identity, and she acted on heaven's directive that day.

From that time nothing would be the same for Mary. Something fundamental took place in her relationship with Jesus. Motherhood faded as discipleship grew. In *The World's First Love,* Bishop Fulton Sheen writes about what he calls the seven laws of love. One of those laws is that "all love, before it mounts to a higher level, must die to a lower one":

At the Marriage Feast in Cana, Mary had an opportunity to keep the love of her Son to herself alone. She had the choice of continuing to be only the Mother of Jesus. But she knew that if she kept that love to herself she would suffer the penalty of never enjoying love to the fullest. If she would save Jesus, she must lose Him. So she asked Him to work His first miracle, to begin His public life, and to anticipate the Hour—and that means His Passion and Death. At that moment, when she asked water to be changed into wine, she died to love of Jesus as her Son and began to mount to the higher love for all whom Jesus would redeem when He died on the cross. Cana was the death of the mother–Son relationship and the beginning of that higher love involved in the . . . Christ-redeemed relationship. And by giving up her Son for the world, she eventually got Him back. . . .[3]

Releasing her son to a public ministry may have involved some uncertainty and even pain for Mary. Yet doing so must have answered her prayers as well, for her mother's heart desired fulfillment of her son's mission. What a mix of emotions she must have experienced! Pride and joy in her son's identity tinged with apprehension as she bore in her soul ominous prophecy.

Are there aspects of her changing relationship with her grown son that can speak to us today?

New Wine

Jesus' new friends had watched, silently, as He visited casually with His mother during the wedding banquet. Clearly Jesus and Mary were devoted to each other; yet why had she said something to Him when the wine ran out? Why didn't she simply keep it to herself? Surely she didn't want to embarrass the host any further.

Jesus seemed to take it personally when Mary told Him about the wine. "Why do you involve me?" He asked. "My time has not yet come."

Mary did not answer Him. She turned instead to the servants. "Do whatever He tells you."

The men who had traveled to Cana with Jesus were mystified. Andrew, Peter, Philip, and Nathanael watched and wondered.

The servants, at Jesus' command, filled six stone jars

with water. Then they drew out a ladleful and poured it into a cup, hurrying to present it to the man hosting the wedding celebration. The host did not realize what had happened; all he knew was that the wine flowing out of the cup he'd been given tasted far superior to the wine served earlier in the evening.

Jesus mingled with the crowd while the four He had brought with Him spoke to one another in amazement.

"John the Baptist believes in Him," one of them remarked. "Now we know why."

Peter felt the most bewildered. "What does all of this mean?" he asked Mary.

Mary was silent for a moment. She had been so careful, so circumspect for all these years about the amazing circumstances and prophecies surrounding Jesus. Loving Him, protecting Him, seeing Him through to maturity had been her life's calling, and she had remained faithful to it always.

But now she sensed that a new time was at hand—perhaps the moment had come for Jesus to lead the Jewish people and assume the throne of David, as the angel Gabriel had foretold. Did she sense the important role Peter would play in her son's calling when she answered? "The Lord's hand has been upon Jesus all His life." She explained His miraculous birth . . . about the shepherds . . . and Simeon's prophecy. . . .

Then Mary paused, waiting to see how Peter would respond. His eyes were alight as he watched Jesus cross the crowded room. "Go on," he said at last. "Tell me everything about Him."

Everything. Mary felt a tug of fear at the back of her mind. The old man in the temple said Jesus would cause the falling and rising of many in Israel—and that many would speak against Him.

Peter nodded. Jesus was laughing. He seemed like any other guest . . . and yet. . . . "I don't understand it all, but I believe the glory of God will be revealed in Jesus," Peter told her.

On her way back to Nazareth, Mary felt apprehensive. A miracle. Now the word about Jesus' powers would begin to spread. And then what would happen? Israel had seldom been kind, even to its greatest prophets. And that was not the half of it: The Roman officials were as nervous as dogs scenting an intruder whenever there was talk of a new leader. Any threat to their rule would become a target of their merciless anger.

Is it finally beginning? Mary prayed silently. If she had never felt caught in events far beyond her power to control, she did so now.

She remained lost in thought. Gray hairs were threaded through her black hair, small lines on her brow deepened.

Lord, I know you have prepared me all along the way for each change in my life—and in Jesus' life. I know I must not hold on to Him too tightly when He needs to be about your business. You have shown me, over and over, your provision for my life, even when the future seemed so uncertain. Yet I feel frightened about what lies ahead. And I am lonely without Joseph. I sense an even deeper loneliness coming. And at the same time, she sensed that Jesus was about to reveal wonderful truths about God.

The conversation she'd had with Jesus in Cana had taken on an odd quality. Mary and Joseph had frequently spoken to Jesus about obedience. She could not count the times she had instructed Him, saying, "Do whatever your father tells you." All at once something was changed. Even as Mary had instructed the servants at Cana, she'd realized with a start that the same instructions applied to her.

Do whatever He tells you.

She must obey her son, just as she had obeyed God all her life.

Mothers and Disciples

Mary faced another choice at this point in her life, and again the Bible suggests she chose the humble path. She yielded herself to selfless discipleship, not knowing what it would bring her personally. The same choice confronts us all, as God's plan for our lives works itself out from day to day. Many times I find I need to resolve in myself to embrace the fulfillment of God's plan for me and for my loved ones, even when there are elements of mystery and risk involved. And—perhaps most poignantly for those of us who are mothers—we must be willing to release our loved ones into God's full will, knowing it may exact a cost upon our own hearts.

Personally, I receive so much encouragement from the example of Mary's conversation with Jesus at Cana. She interceded as a mother and as a disciple. As a mother, her words to Jesus provide a model for all mothers as they seek to direct their children without coercing them. Rare is the mother who can hold her tongue when she perceives a direction her child needs to take. Our natural inclination is to say, "Get with it. Do it this way."

Mary's approach was subtle, and very effective. She and Jesus must have had an open, empathetic line of communication between them, so that Mary simply had to point out what was needed. Jesus knew instantly that Mary was suggesting, without ever saying so, that He should take responsibility for putting the situation right.

Yet Mary, by this time, was becoming something other

than Jesus' mother. She was also His disciple. And as a disciple she interceded with Him, just as we can today through prayer. Her influence at Cana confirms intercession's power, and its significance even in the most routine matters of everyday life.

When she interceded, Jesus responded, "It is not my time." Yet Mary instructed the servants to obey Jesus' directions. Mary had spoken with her son, and now she would step back and leave the rest to Him.

The *Complete Biblical Library* explains that Mary's response recognizes proper authority. When He was twelve, Jesus knew who He was. Still, He submitted to parental authority. At Cana, the time arrived when He was subject only to God, and Mary recognized Jesus' authority over her.[4]

In this brief biblical passage, Mary models for us a pattern for prayer. She is not hesitant about pointing out a situation that needs to be remedied—even though it is a relatively minor concern. God cares about the details of our lives—even about the way in which we entertain guests! There is nothing so insignificant that it cannot be brought before the Lord in prayer.

This passage also teaches us that God answers prayer. He responds, even if the response may not be what we expect, desire, or even feel we deserve. Sometimes it seems to take a deposit of prayer to build, and then God moves—sometimes after what seems like a long, long time. Yet no prayer is wasted.

I do not think, as some have suggested, that Mary felt rebuffed or confused at Jesus' first response. This mother knew her son's heart. She did not give the Lord orders about what to do and how to do it. She expressed the need, and would rest in His response, whatever it would be.

After she interceded with Jesus, she told the servants in simple faith, "Do whatever He tells you." In these, the last recorded words of Mary in Scripture, we are supplied with the most perfect set of instructions any believer could hope to receive: Do *whatever the Lord tells you—do it.*

Fulton Sheen beautifully expands on this thought:

> Our wills are ours only to give away. The human heart is torn between a sense of emptiness and a need for being filled, like the waterpots of Cana. The emptiness comes from the fact that we are human. The power of filling belongs only to Him Who ordered the waterpots filled. Lest any heart should fail in being filled, Mary's last valedictory is: "Whatsoever He shall say to you, that do ye." The heart has a need of emptying and a need of being filled. The power of emptying is human—emptying in the love of others—the power of filling belongs only to God. Hence all perfect love must end on the note: "Not my will, but Thine be done, O Lord!"[5]

Questions to Ponder

1. What does it mean for me today to make a choice for selfless discipleship? Am I willing to move ahead in God's plan for my life regardless of my natural uncertainty?
2. How effective is my prayer life? What are some of the things going on in my life that need to be brought to the Lord's attention?
3. When I pray, do I order God around or do I humbly point out to Him the situations that need attention? How can my prayer life more closely resemble Mary's

model of intercession at Cana?

4. Am I ready to do whatever He tells me? What do I believe God is telling me now, and how can I best fulfill His plan obediently?

*T*hen Jesus entered a house, and again a crowd gathered, so that he and his disciples were not even able to eat. When his family heard about this, they went to take charge of him, for they said, "He is out of his mind."

And the teachers of the law who came down from Jerusalem said, "He is possessed by Beelzebub! By the prince of demons he is driving out demons."

Then Jesus' mother and brothers arrived. Standing outside, they sent someone in to call him. A crowd was sitting around him, and they told him, "Your mother and brothers are outside looking for you."

"Who are my mother and my brothers?" he asked. Then he looked at those seated in a circle around him and said, "Here are my mother and my brothers! Whoever does God's will is my brother and sister and mother."

MARK 3:20–22; 31–35

As Jesus was saying these things, a woman in the crowd called out, "Blessed is the mother who gave you birth and nursed you."

He replied, "Blessed rather are those who hear the word of God and obey it."

LUKE 11:27, 28

9

Our True Family

AFTER JESUS CALLED His first disciples and changed water into wine at Cana, His ministry expanded at a rapid pace. To Mary and others who knew Jesus well, it must have seemed as if His very identity had changed overnight. Something in His pace made it seem that He was making up for lost time. After thirty years of silence and studied obscurity, He emerged with the intensity of the morning sun—preaching throughout the land, healing people, holding crowds spellbound with vivid parables about God's kingdom, all the while challenging the accepted wisdom of the Jewish religious hierarchy.

No wonder Mary felt uncomfortable about all the attention her son attracted—so anxious, in fact, that she felt a need to go and see for herself. What danger did she sense as the scribes and Pharisees publicly criticized everything

Jesus said? By this time, Mary was approaching what we would call middle-age, and is believed to have been widowed. No doubt she was dependent upon the men in her family for support. As far as we know, her major life's work had consisted of rearing Jesus, protecting Him, nurturing and training Him in all the knowledge of the law and the prophets. And so to feel strongly protective of any threat against her son must have come naturally to Mary.

The Bible records an incident that occurred most probably at Peter's house in Capernaum, on the northern shore of the Sea of Galilee. In that small fishing village, where Jesus lived at the time, He found His first disciples, Simon Peter and Andrew, casting their fishing nets into the water. Jesus no doubt found security at the home of Peter, particularly when He'd fallen under the cold scrutiny of the religious community. On this occasion, the scribes from Jerusalem were after Him, accusing Him of being in league with the Devil.

Immediately, too, Jesus had drawn a landslide of attention from sick, handicapped, and demonized people. His healing abilities had become legendary. Even in this seaside sanctuary, Jesus was unable to escape the surging crowds of people seeking relief. Perhaps His family was attempting to get Jesus out of the spotlight and back home to Nazareth for a time to let things settle down.

Today, what remains of ancient Capernaum consists of carefully excavated and preserved ruins. Visiting an archeological dig there, I was intrigued by the remains of the ancient synagogue. Built in the second or third century, the structure reflects the Greco-Roman architectural style, but is decorated in Jewish motif. Since Jews built new synagogues on the sites of old ones, Jesus quite likely preached in the original synagogue at that very site. It may have been on this spot that He healed the servant of the centurion who built the synagogue, as Luke 7:2–10 tells us. Workers had recently uncovered a portion of the original synagogue floor, reportedly dating from the time of Jesus. Near the Capernaum synagogue lay the low ruins of a first-century house, which archaeologists contend was Peter's home. It stood near the banks of the sea where He fished for a living. The synagogue was beyond His home, inland several hundred feet.

There is a group of theologians who believe that the account of Mary and other family members coming to call Jesus home reveals that they had lost faith in Jesus and His mission. They contend His family was intent on stopping Him—yet this view contradicts everything I have learned about Mary. Is it consistent to think that Mary, who persevered through so many trials for the sake of her son, would suddenly change her mind and try to hinder His work? If not, then how can we understand why she went boldly with the others when they tried to get in touch with Him?

On the face of things, women tend to be peacemakers. Women dislike conflict and violence more than most men. Our Creator implanted in us a mother's heart, whose nurturing instinct wants to make peace. Women can often be the fixers of the world. We try to right wrong relationships and mend broken hearts. When children are young, mothers fix their hurts with bandages and kisses: They minister to body and soul. And for most of us women, the mothering instinct remains intact no matter how many years go by. This is a great gift, despite the fact that it makes us more vulnerable to heartbreak and more subject to abuse.

Mary—every bit a human mother—would want to be available when Jesus needed her, to pour soothing oil on the troubled circumstances Jesus encountered. Mary went, I am convinced, not out of unbelief in Jesus and His ministry, but as a peacemaker. If there was agitation among the family about the controversial nature of Jesus' ministry Mary would calm it. I can only imagine what thoughts may have crossed her mind as events swirled around her.

Always a Mother

Mary's mind churned as she and several other family members walked along a pathway through a valley known as the Wadi of the Doves, on their way to Capernaum. *Why do I have such a disagreement within my own feelings? I've longed for Jesus to walk the road you have prepared for Him. Yet I am so afraid when the leaders attack Him!* As they reached the Sea of Galilee, Mary looked out over the water, its smooth blue expansiveness calming her spirit.

I had to come here—for Him, she told herself. *The family has been so upset—some of them even want to take Him away by force, if they have to. We've heard so many rumors. I know they mean well. They fear for Jesus' life—but I know they are embarrassed by Him, too. They whisper that He's insane! If Jesus would only declare himself and His true mission openly. . . . Why does He keep it to himself?*

The crowd surrounding Peter's dwelling stood ten deep. Many more people milled in the street, having given up hope of reaching Jesus. No one recognized Mary here. For that she was thankful, fearing she might be besieged by the crowd if they knew she was His mother. They might think she could coax Him into doing some special personal favor.

Surrounded by those with whom she had traveled, Mary saw Andrew, one of Jesus' first disciples who had accompanied Him to Cana not long ago. She motioned to him urgently. "Andrew, please tell Jesus we are here. We must speak with Him."

Andrew threaded his way through the crowd, and Mary drew closer, as close as she could in order to catch a glimpse of her son through a door or window. There He was! He was standing in a far corner of the room, with people clustered at His feet and packed throughout the house.

One of Jesus' kinsmen—highly skeptical about all that had happened in recent months—surveyed the scene with disbelief. "Why doesn't He tell them plainly He is no new prophet? Who does He think He is?"

Andrew reached Jesus and delivered the message. Jesus nodded His head but made no motion toward coming outside. *He is just standing there,* Mary thought. She strained to hear what He would say, and the crowd quieted as Jesus stood up to speak.

"Who are my mother and my brothers?" he called out loudly—not so much in answer to the question, but using the question as the beginning point from which to bring some truth to light. "*Here* are my mother and my brothers!" Jesus said, indicating the very people sitting in the crowded room—people who, for the most part, Jesus had never met before. "Whoever does God's will is my brother and my sister and my mother."

Mary could not bring herself to look at their kinsmen. And the one who was most critical was quick to react to Jesus' words. "There," he said triumphantly. "Jesus is going to ignore us. He's gotten so swept up in all this acclaim that He disowns us publicly. This is to His shame."

Mary held her thoughts calmly. "Come," she said to a young nephew with her, "let's go down by the shore."

The little group from Nazareth left the crowd behind and walked along the sand, and Mary held her tongue until they were well out of earshot. "There are a few things we need to remember," Mary said patiently but resolutely. "Jesus is doing exactly what God has sent Him to do . . . from the time He was a baby He was meant for this. Just because it is all happening so fast, and just because He hasn't told us every detail—that is no reason to question Him or call Him crazy. I long to talk with Him, spend time alone with Him—to understand. But everything is different now, and we need to trust Him."

The others stood silently. They permitted her to have the last word—after all, she was His mother. And, deep inside, they hoped she was right. Jesus made friends with tax collectors, lepers, the dregs of society; and He shook the very foundations of religious and human complacency everywhere He went. It was unspeakably frustrating, embarrassing—even dangerous—to be associated with Jesus and His teachings these days. Yet there was something so authentic about Him, so genuine. . . . The relatives set their jaws in silence, if for no other reason than to honor Mary.

But in her heart, Mary had many more questions than she allowed to be seen on the surface. *God, no matter what anyone thinks or says, I want you to know that whatever your plan is for Jesus and for me, I say yes to it! Just stay very close to us, for it's a frightening thing that unfolds before us.*

New Relationships

This incident in Capernaum occurred not long after Mary had witnessed a profound change in her son Jesus. Scattered to the wind were all the things she used to take for granted: His regular hours of working as a carpenter, His availability, perhaps even His financial provision for her. In the twinkling of an eye, beginning with Jesus' baptism in the Jordan River, all the constants in Mary's life vanished.

In their place, gnawing uncertainty must have mingled with a sense of dawning fulfillment as Mary watched her son step out confidently and swiftly into the tasks and purposes ordained for Him. All at once, Jesus became widely known and sought-after. Crowds trailed His every move, and the demands for His healing and comfort intensified. And that was not all. Jesus attracted hostile attention as well, and from the most exalted religious leaders among the Jews.

The uneasiness Jesus' family must have felt was fueled by the comments of others. In the incident at Capernaum, some of the scribes are quoted as saying Jesus was possessed by demons, and that He cast out demons by the power of the Evil One. Surely Mary, of all people, knew this was ludicrously false. Yet all of us are influenced, to some extent, by secondhand comments, hearsay, even outright gossip that we hear about others. Our opinions and attitudes, our fears and human reactions are shaped to some extent by innuendo so subtle we do not even recognize it consciously. Particularly if the stray comments involve our children or other loved ones, we feel almost compelled to respond swiftly and decisively.

Mary did not sit back and listen to accusations about Jesus. She went out of her way to go to Him with other family members who had been influenced by the criticisms, and she tried to set the record straight directly. Surely, there is a lesson here for every one of us coping with imperfect relationships today: When we find ourselves perplexed about a person we love, we need to approach them with open minds and open hearts. We need to hear what they truly are saying, and not accept hurtful characterizations put forward by others.

Mary's concern is evident in this passage—evident in the urgency with which she and the others sought Jesus out and called for Him to come and see them immediately. Many mothers of grown children will understand Mary's emotional turmoil. It is natural for us to have expectations for our children—to envision what they will be doing, how they will behave—when they are adults. And then the reality often does not match our personal fantasy.

When our children decide to march to the beat of a different drummer, how do we respond? Are we able to keep on supporting and loving them unconditionally?

Mary sought Jesus out when questions arose about what He was doing. So often our inclination is to stay put, and close down communication when we feel hurt, slighted, or neglected by a child. Mary did not succumb to this sort of destructive self-pity. As she had throughout her life, she placed her son's needs ahead of her own, and went to find out for herself what He was doing; to stand with Him and be there if He needed her.

Having taken the first step, how must Mary have felt when He would not come out and see her? We do not know what she said or did, because the Bible only tells us what Jesus said. Apparently, no major scene occurred; no one tried to drag Jesus bodily out of the house He was visiting. Jesus responded to Mary's request in a way that some interpret as callous and negligent. Obviously, there is more going on here than meets the eye.

As the Lord of us all, Jesus used this opportunity to teach us the ultimate importance of being part of His Father's spiritual, eternal family. In doing so, He made it clear that He is equally available to all who believe in Him—no one can claim to be more Christian than someone else because of a first-class relationship with Him (not even

His blood relatives). When He heard His mother and brothers were outside, Jesus did not accord them any special privileges of access. Instead, He directed His remarks to the crowd, asking, "Who are my mother and my brothers?" His message: All believers who do God's will are a part of the eternal family of God. Anyone who is faithful to God's will are Jesus' brothers and sisters and mother.

Author C. Milo Connick comments on this incident:

> The meaning is clear. The supreme relationship in life is not biological; it is spiritual. The kingdom of God has top priority. All other attachments—even the most intimate and personal—are secondary.[1]

Jesus was teaching that earthly relationships are superseded by spiritual relationships. It is of eternal consequence to be inside the Christian community, and not outside looking in.

For Mary, personally, this was one more point where she must choose to release her child to fulfill His life's mission. The change in their relationship could not be controlled as He moved out boldly in public ministry.

At another point, Jesus would emphatically show that all believers have equal access to Him. Luke records an incident in which a woman in the crowd cried out in exuberance, "Blessed is the mother who gave you birth and nursed you."

Jesus responded, "Blessed rather are those who hear the word of God and obey it!" (see Luke 11:27, 28). The source of Mary's great blessing was not her physical relationship to Jesus, but her spiritual one.

What effect does this have on us today? I believe it brings Mary closer to us and makes her choices and attitudes even more relevant to the matters we struggle with.

Jesus confirms in this passage that *everyone* who hears and obeys can enjoy a close, personal relationship with Him. Drawing near to Jesus does not hinge on earthly measures of self-worth—our family name, for example, or how well-educated we are, the neighborhood we come from, or our level of income.

Nor does the Lord want us to focus on Christian personalities. In this media age, the world responds to celebrities. Some in the church imitate the world and follow celebrity leaders in ministry. They do this rather than giving full attention to Jesus, the One upon whom those ministries are based.

Listening to what others say about Jesus' life and teachings is helpful—but it can never replace our need to live out our faith. We have the incredible privilege of listening directly to the Lord himself, by communing with Him personally in prayer and through His Word. He can speak to our hearts as we worship Him with other believers, read the Bible and pray, and get involved in Bible studies and discussions of God's Word. While many preachers, evangelists, and authors serve God faithfully and illuminate His Word, we may run the risk of exalting particular ministries and personalities rather than the Lord if we rely only on "popular" leaders for our spiritual care and feeding.

There is another facet of Mary's character that shines through in the story of Jesus in the crowded house. She knew there were harsh opinions of Jesus emanating even from His own family, but she did not sit back, toss up her hands in despair, and let things go from bad to worse. Mary went out of her way to try to restore a broken relationship. Many women are truly peacemakers, particularly in the home.

Bishop Fulton Sheen, in identifying some differences

between men and women, makes the following observations:

> The man governs the home, but the woman reigns. Government is related to justice; reigning is related to love. . . . The man is normally more serene than the woman, more absorbent of the daily shocks of life, less disturbed by trifles. But on the other hand, in the great crises of life it is the woman who, because of her gentle power of reigning, can give great consolation to man in his troubles. When he is remorseful, sad, and disquieted, she brings comfort and assurance. As the surface of the ocean is agitated and troubled, but the great depths are calm, so in the really great catastrophes that affect the soul, the woman is the depth and the man is the surface.[2]

I believe Mary stood at Peter's door in Capernaum as a reconciler. She faced an unpleasant situation head-on, pouring healing balm on the problem. Mary had the heart of a peacemaker.

Today we need peacemakers—not those who only talk of peace, but those who minister true and abiding peace to individuals, even when it means venturing into the middle of outward conflict.

True peace comes through Mary's son, the "Prince of Peace." Like Mary, we who have received the peace that passes all understanding are called to take Jesus' healing love to troubled individuals everywhere that we may find them—and that means starting in our own families.

Questions to Ponder

1. Are changes occurring in any of my most significant relationships today? How do I feel about these changes?

2. If I am feeling hurt or confused by these changes, what steps can I take before the Lord to restore the relationship? How does Mary's example at Capernaum speak to my circumstances?

3. Do I find myself being unduly influenced by the opinions of others or by those who are elevated to celebrity status in the church? Have I tested those opinions or teachings against the Word of God?

4. In what ways is God calling me to be a peacemaker in my home, my extended family, the Body of Christ, my neighborhood, or my community?

*F*inally Pilate handed him over to them to be crucified. So the soldiers took charge of Jesus. Carrying his own cross, he went out to the Place of the Skull (which in Aramaic is called Golgotha). Here they crucified him, and with him two others—one on each side and Jesus in the middle.

JOHN 19:16–18

Jesus said, "Father, forgive them, for they do not know what they are doing." And they divided up his clothes by casting lots.

The people stood watching, and the rulers even sneered at him. They said, "He saved others; let him save himself if he is the Christ of God, the Chosen One."

LUKE 23:34, 35

Pilate had a notice prepared and fastened to the cross. It read: Jesus of Nazareth, the King of the Jews. Many of the Jews read this sign, for the place where Jesus was crucified was near the city, and the sign was written in Aramaic, Latin, and Greek.

Near the cross of Jesus stood his mother, his mother's sister, Mary the wife of Clopas, and Mary of Magdala. When Jesus saw his mother there, and the disciple whom he loved standing nearby, he said to his mother, "Dear woman, here is your son," and to the disciple, "Here is your mother." From that time on, this disciple took her into his home.

JOHN 19:19, 20; 25–27

10

The Sword Pierces

TODAY, THE ANCIENT CITY of Jerusalem remains steeped in the mystery of Jesus' passion and resurrection. You can sense it as you walk through the old city, with its narrow, winding ways and Eastern markets. On the traditional site of the Lord's death, burial, and resurrection stands the massive Church of the Holy Sepulchre. It marks the end of the *Via Dolorosa*, a Latin name meaning "Way of Sorrow." This is the route that tradition says Jesus took to Golgotha, a site used for Roman executions known as Calvary. Pilgrims who visit Jerusalem still walk along the Way of Sorrow, following in the footsteps of their Lord and Savior.

Not far away is the site the Jews consider holiest in all Jerusalem: a portion of the western wall of the temple, which for centuries has served as the focal point of Israeli national life. It was at the temple in Jerusalem that the birth of John the Baptist was announced; it was where Mary and Joseph offered the required sacrificial offering for the birth of their firstborn son. Inside the temple, Simeon and Anna confirmed to Mary the identity and the significance of her new baby boy; and it was where the worried parents found twelve-year-old Jesus deep in dialogue with the rabbis.

After the wedding at Cana, Jesus visited the temple at Jerusalem and discovered men there selling cattle, sheep, and doves. With a whip He drove them out and scattered the coins of the money changers. When the Jewish leaders demanded to know on what authority He did this, Jesus replied, "Destroy this temple, and I will raise it again in three days" (John 2:13–19). Now we know what they could not grasp—that Jesus was referring to His impending crucifixion and resurrection.

We can only imagine the memories Jerusalem held for Mary as she waited there, observing Passover and wondering what would happen to her son. That week brought to fulfillment the purpose for which God called Mary some thirty-four years before. What was she doing as public sentiment turned so viciously against Jesus? Was she there on the day commemorated by many as Palm Sunday, when the people triumphantly hailed Jesus as He rode into the city on a donkey? Did she follow in the crowd of admirers? We do not know.

Surely Mary had heard that Jesus raised Lazarus from the dead. She must have known about His many healings and how He multiplied five loaves of bread to feed thousands of people gathered to hear Him teach. She probably knew He had spent a great deal of time in prayer and that recently, after an agonizing time of prayer, He had been placed under arrest. Did she know what Jesus said when He was taken before Pilate? "You are right in saying

I am a king," Jesus had told the skeptical leader. "In fact, for this reason I was born, and for this I came into the world, to testify to the truth. Everyone on the side of truth listens to me."

If she kept track of all Jesus said and did, Mary knew how deeply He threatened the religious leaders. Had she heard from the disciples about their last supper with Jesus? Did the disciples tell Mary about Jesus' agony in the garden as he sweat blood in the anguish of knowing what He faced? We cannot say for certain.

We do know that Mary witnessed the awful events herself, and remained steadfastly near Him through it all. It is difficult to overstate the gruesomeness of crucifixion. In *Jesus, the Man, the Mission, the Message*, it is described this way:

> Crucifixion . . . was a punishment reserved for rebels, slaves, and criminals of the lowest classes. . . . The condemned person was first scourged, a brutally painful experience in itself. As part of his punishment he was forced to carry the heavy crossbeam . . . which weighed about eighty or ninety pounds, to the place of execution. . . .
>
> The place of execution was as public as possible, usually by some well-traveled road. It thus served as a grim warning to witnesses not to provoke "the governing authorities" (Romans 13:1). When the condemned reached his destination, he was stripped of his clothing. His hands were nailed or tied to the ends of the crossbeam. Then he was lifted up and fastened to a permanent upright pole or post. His body was supported on the pole by a block, his legs were lashed out in an unnatural position, and his feet were nailed or his ankles tied to the upright post so that they were a few inches off the ground. Exposure, loss of blood,

maltreatment by sadistic spectators, torture by insects, and impaired circulation caused excruciating pain. Death was normally welcomed as a friend after about twelve hours, but men sometimes suffered for much longer periods.[1]

Can you imagine the scene? Jews had traveled to Jerusalem from far and wide for the Passover. Throngs of people crowded into the city, and the chief topic of conversation was this man many called the "King of the Jews." When Jesus was crucified, a mob of curiosity-seekers undoubtedly joined His detractors and supporters to witness His death.

And Mary, as the end approached, finally experienced the moment anticipated so long ago by wise old Simeon: It was as if a sword pierced her very soul as she watched her son die in pain and torment.

"Why Have You Forsaken Me?"

At Golgotha, Mary could only watch in anguish as a contingent of Roman soldiers lashed Jesus' wrists to the cross and nailed His feet. They were so practiced and business-like that the whole procedure took only minutes. Jesus spoke haltingly in His agony, and Mary heard Him: "Father, forgive them for they do not know what they are doing."

Sobs racked her body. If only she could take the nails instead of her son—the physical pain could be no worse than her agony of soul. *This is what Simeon said would happen!* she thought. *It is more than I can bear.*

O my God, she prayed, *as they drove the nails into Jesus' hands and feet, it was as if they drove them into my heart. How can they hate Him like this? He hangs there without a* shred—naked before them all—bleeding, beaten, spat upon. And they laugh at His pain. . . .

The agony went on for hours, and through it all Mary stood there, immovable, unable to comfort the son she had cherished and protected so diligently from the moment she conceived Him.

The sky grew dark. In the distance, thunder rumbled. At last, Jesus cried out, "My God, my God, why have you forsaken me?"

Mary could not restrain her sobs. She began pleading with God anew. *He is crying out to you, Lord. Hear Him! Don't let Him suffer any more.*

Then Mary's knees grew weak. She had to steady herself on the arm of one of the women who had remained with her. There they stood, these faithful women, holding each other a short distance from that instrument of death.

Lightning flashed. The air had grown oppressive. Now Mary forced herself to look up into Jesus' swollen face. He was looking directly at her, sweat and tears coursing down His bloodied cheeks. Beneath the pain was the flame of love! Forcing the words out through dry and swollen lips required a monumental effort, but Jesus looked from Mary to John and said, "Dear woman, here is your son," and then, to John, "Here is your mother."

For a few more hideous moments, Jesus' body was racked with convulsive heaves. Then He cried to heaven, "It is finished."

Terrible darkness shrouded Golgotha and Jerusalem. The women near Mary wept for Jesus—and they ached for the mother He loved.

Mary walked bravely to the cross though a Roman soldier stepped forward as if to prevent her. One soldier was breaking the legs of the other two victims. A third, seeing Jesus was dead already, thrust a sword into His side. Blood and water spilled from the wound. Simeon's words shouted in Mary's heart with gruesome finality. *A sword shall pierce your soul.*

Mary clung to the rough, wooden upright cross. John had followed her and stood there silently with one hand on her shoulder, allowing her a moment of solitary grief. Mary wept, and wept . . . as rain drenched the whole sad scene.

When the rain ended, Joseph of Arimathea, Nicodemus, and the others took Jesus' body from the cross and covered His naked form. Mary was numb, her face ashen. *I just have to touch Him one more time,* she thought, *to hold Him.* The others seemed to read her thoughts and understood. Time was short, for they had to bury the body before sundown, but they stood back and let the woman say goodbye to her son.

Mary struggled awkwardly to hold the limp body, managing to pull Jesus onto her lap as she half-knelt and half-sat in the blood-spattered dirt and mud. She rocked Him gently, as she had so many times when He was young.

"I love you," she whispered, surveying the gentle, marred face. His hair was matted—His beard partially pulled out—His face distorted. Looking up, Mary said softly, "You have Him now, God." Then reluctantly, she released the broken, lifeless body.

She was spent.

The End, and the Beginning

Inevitably, suffering invades the life of every believer, just as it did Mary's life. Suffering is particularly acute when it involves our children—those precious ones we have cared for since they were newborns. In the Bible, Mary was not the first parent of whom God requested the ultimate sacrifice.

The temple in Jerusalem marked the place where, some 2,000 years before, the Lord asked Abraham to sacrifice his child of promise, Isaac, on the altar (see Genesis 22). Abraham had a covenant relationship with God. He was committed to doing God's will, and God was committed to care for Abraham and fulfill His promises. When directed, Abraham relinquished his beloved son to God's will.

God tested Abraham's obedience, but in the end He didn't require Abraham to sacrifice his precious Isaac. God provided a different sacrifice—a ram caught in a nearby thicket. On that black day at Calvary, there was no last-minute substitution for the sacrifice God required. Mary's son *was* God's chosen sacrifice. Jesus was Mary's offering that day. When God gave His Son for us, Mary gave her son, too. A great lesson of relinquishment is implicit in the crucifixion. Releasing our loved ones into our Father's hands is extremely difficult. Most of us wrestle with it, yet it is one of our greatest acts of love toward them and toward God. Removing our hands of interference from our loved ones opens a clearer path on which God may move in their lives, influenced by our faith and our prayers. Mary, by her conduct at the cross, gives us an exemplary model of godly relinquishment.

That day at Calvary, pivotal for all eternity, Jesus suffered the ultimate rejection, by the very people He came to save. Yet Mary stood with Him, as both mother and disciple. I believe she was strengthened by all the ways in which God had prepared her through the years. From the time of His birth, she could see that Jesus drew the wrath of the ungodly. She and Joseph had to flee with Him into Egypt to avoid Herod's crazed order to kill infant boys. They had to begin relinquishing Him to God's purposes when He was twelve and stayed behind at the temple.

Mary identified with Jesus in triumph and in tragedy. Perhaps the hardest thing to bear, besides Jesus' physical suffering, was the cruel mockery dealt Him by the leaders as well as the common people. There is something almost unbearable about seeing our children attacked and ridiculed, not for what they do, but for *who they are*. How do we respond at times like these? If our children are in need of correction, at any age, we need to discern that and help bring about change. Yet if our children, or others we love, are falsely accused we may learn much from Mary's example. Above all else, Mary stayed right beside Jesus. She stood by Him, even when many of His own disciples and other followers fled in fear and confusion. We, too, may face unsettling moments in the lives of those we love. Yet we are called to stick with them, being present to permit God to use us in the best way possible to bring healing, peace, comfort, or resolution. In this, we need to put their welfare before our own pride and emotional comfort.

As Jesus grew from infancy into boyhood and finally into maturity, Mary must have suspected that a time of grim confrontation lay ahead. She probably did not know just what would happen, or when, but perhaps she anticipated some great crisis. How can any of us imagine the anguish of watching your own child being crucified? Any normal mother would try to stop it. I would have tried to pull the soldiers away. I would have screamed for justice. But Mary did not. Jesus was a lamb led to the slaughter in meek submission. Mary watched the slaughter—silent and submissive.

Meekness in our contemporary society carries a connotation of weakness, yet when the Lord said, "Blessed are the meek, for they shall inherit the earth," He meant those who are gentle, patient, and long-suffering (Matthew 5:5). Meekness is power under control.

The cross must have threatened Mary with incapacitating loneliness. Joseph was gone, and though others tried to help, she stood alone in her sorrow. Yet, embodied in her singular role was great honor. Mary was the only one privileged to be present at both Jesus' birth and death. When we feel lonely and abandoned, we should consider what God required of Mary. Yet He gave her grace to endure and to emerge triumphant.

In our circumstances, do we draw on His all-sufficient grace (2 Corinthians 12:9)? Grace is undeserved favor—a blessing we have not earned and do not deserve, but is freely given by a God who loves us.

On that day of great humiliation, the relationship between Jesus and Mary, which had been changing over the years, took on a deeper dimension. Her son was also her Savior, and she had watched Him die a death that purchased her salvation. Jesus did not spare even His own mother from suffering.

She was His mother, and at the cross Jesus gave special attention to her care, giving her into the protection of His beloved disciple John. As a mother I am touched that in the midst of His suffering, Jesus thought of His mom.

Jesus also indicated a special sensitivity toward other women who faithfully stood by as He was crucified. On the way to the cross, He turned to them and said, "Daughters of Jerusalem, do not weep for me. Weep for yourselves and for your children. For the time will come when you will say, 'Blessed are the barren women, the wombs that never bore and the breasts that never nursed!' . . . For if men do these things when the tree is green, what will happen when it is dry?" (Luke 23:28–31). In saying this, Jesus offered a glimpse into the future that awaited the people of Israel as well as His followers through the ages. Entering into a relationship with Jesus means suffering some rejection, even persecution, for the sake of His name. Yet His love for us is not conditioned upon the vastness of our faith; nor should our faith be conditioned on God's favors bestowed on us.

At the cross we find faithful women. Most of the men fled in fear or disappointment. Jesus' special friend John was there, but most of the men were not nearby. They recognized not only the pain and humiliation but also the danger of the moment. Yet the women endured, allowing themselves to be identified with their broken, bleeding Savior.

There is something special about the determined tenacity of a woman who takes a stand of commitment. It is an attribute of the mother's heart of woman. The Scriptures do not record any instance where a woman failed Jesus during His life on earth. That is not to say none did, or that women are more reliable than men. Perhaps women's failings are often more subtle than men's. Yet it had to please the Lord that the faithful women were with Him until it was finished.

At the end, Joseph of Arimathea and the others hurriedly prepared Jesus' body for burial. Mary must have watched intently as they readied Him for the tomb. At His birth Mary wrapped His tiny body in the swaddling clothes of a newborn. At His death they wrapped the pallid form in the linen of the dead. It appeared to be the end of Jesus and His ministry. In truth, we know it was just the beginning.

Questions to Ponder

1. If you are a parent, what does relinquishment mean to you? Have you faced the necessity of relinquishing a child? How did you prepare for it ahead of time?
2. Put yourself in Mary's place. At what point during Jesus' passion and crucifixion would your reserves of faith and trust have been most sorely tested?
3. How has God helped prepare you for times when you were required to persevere, and not give up?

*O*n the evening of that first day of the week, when the disciples were together, with the doors locked for fear of the Jews, Jesus came and stood among them and said, "Peace be with you!" After he said this, he showed them his hands and side. The disciples were overjoyed when they saw the Lord.

JOHN 20:19–20

On one occasion, while he was eating with them, he gave them this command: "Do not leave Jerusalem, but wait for the gift my Father promised, which you have heard me speak about. For John baptized with water, but in a few days you will be baptized with the Holy Spirit."

So when they met together, they asked him, "Lord, are you this time going to restore the kingdom to Israel?" He said to them, "It is not for you to know the times or dates the Father has set by his own authority. But you will receive power when the Holy Spirit comes on you; and you will be my witnesses in Jerusalem, and in all Judea and Samaria, and to the ends of the earth."

After he said this, he was taken up before their very eyes, and a cloud hid him from their sight. They were looking intently up into the sky as he was going, when suddenly two men dressed in white stood beside them.

"Men of Galilee," they said, "why do you stand here looking into the sky? This same Jesus, who has been taken from you into heaven, will come back in the same way you have seen him go into heaven."

Then they returned to Jerusalem. . . . They all joined together constantly in prayer, along with the women and Mary the mother of Jesus, and his brothers.

ACTS 1:4–14

Sent

In between the intense grief of the cross and the explosive joy of Pentecost comes a period of time that offers much substance for reflection. After Jesus died came three agonizing days before His resurrection. This mirrors the three days of waiting Mary and Joseph experienced as they sought their missing son in Jerusalem. The time between Jesus' death and resurrection was the second three-day period in which His mother prayed, in grief and anguish, over His absence.

I don't believe Mary ever lost faith in Jesus' return, but she probably didn't understand how it would occur. She must have laughed and cried when Mary Magdalene came running from the empty tomb, eyes wide with tears of excitement.

Remember the words her cousin Elizabeth spoke years before? "Blessed is she who has believed that what the Lord has said to her will be accomplished!" The Lord's message through Gabriel had at last come to fullness. By conquering death, Jesus now reigned in a way that transcended the finite political expectations people had for Him. His kingdom—alive in the hearts of individuals who believe in Him—would never end.

For forty blessed days, the risen Jesus lived and moved again among His friends, impressing upon them the fact of what had happened and preparing them for the difficult challenges ahead. Mary knew Jesus didn't leave His followers without instructions. He told them, "Therefore go and make disciples of all nations, baptizing them in the name of the Father and of the Son and of the Holy Spirit, and teaching them to obey everything I commanded you. And surely I will be with you always, to the very end of the age" (Matthew 28:19, 20).

But how would they accomplish this? Most of them scarcely mustered enough energy to pray with Jesus the night of His arrest, or the courage to stay with Him through His ordeal on the cross.

There could be only one way for this command to be fulfilled. . . .

The Holy Spirit stirred the complacent water of their souls "like the blowing of a violent wind" (Acts 2:2). The Bible describes a stunning scene: "They saw what seemed to be tongues of fire that separated and came to rest on each of them. All of them were filled with the Holy Spirit and began to speak in other tongues as the Spirit enabled them" (Acts 2:3, 4). Jews from every nation could hear the message of Jesus in their native tongues. And Peter, once as unsettled as the sea, began to lead the believers with newfound strength and conviction.

For all this, Mary was present. The gospels do not

depict her as seeking any special attention. She was just one of the faithful who would pray and wait as Jesus directed. At Pentecost, Mary joined the Spirit-filled disciples of her Savior and son. Along with His other disciples, she was committed to this new, explosive movement.

Through her decades with Jesus, she certainly knew the risks associated with following Him. For this new movement, primarily as a vehicle to change Judaism from within, many uncertainties lay ahead.

Mary was the only woman there whose name is identified in Scripture. She was Jesus' disciple. Luci Shaw puts it this way:

> After the Resurrection and Ascension of Jesus, Mary found her rightful place in the upper room (Acts 1:14) with the others of His inner circle, equally joined with them in the risk and intimacy of prayer, the responsibility for the young church. By faithfulness she had demonstrated her value to God and to His "sent ones." Her suffering had been redemptive.[1]

Pentecost marked the first time the Holy Spirit came upon Peter and the others in such great power. It was, however, the second time the Holy Spirit came upon Mary. He had, of course, inspired her prophetic words in the Magnificat and kept her through her life's trials. However, the Holy Spirit first came upon Mary when she was a young virgin, overshadowing her and causing the Son of God to be conceived in her womb by His power.

What happened to Mary after that exciting day of Pentecost? She is never again mentioned in Scripture. Some scholars believe Mary lived ten or twenty years after Jesus ascended to heaven. We don't know, however, what she did during that time—how long she lived, exactly where, except that she was in the care of John. He must have drawn much encouragement and understanding from Mary as she shared Jesus with him as only His mother could. Some believe Mary died in Jerusalem. On the other hand, *The Communicator's Commentary* theorizes that she lived with John in his exile on Patmos, a tiny island in the Aegean Sea between Turkey and Crete.

Throughout Mary's life she persevered in faith, holding fast to the vision God gave her. Her reward was profound—even lavish—and it is the very same reward available to all believers today. Jesus, who once was born of Mary's womb, was reborn in her heart. At Pentecost, Mary experienced new birth in Christ, her Lord and Savior. After the death and resurrection of her son Jesus, Mary continued to have, at the very center of her life, a vital relationship with Him.

Power from On High

Together, Mary and John walked along the uneven paving stones toward the temple courts, where the Lord's disciples had agreed to meet. In their silent camaraderie, Mary remembered the pain of those three dark days after the Crucifixion. *I could never explain to anyone the agony of those days,* Mary thought. *O my God, faith in you never left me—but my heart felt so broken.* And she thought of the small shattered band of disciples Jesus had left behind.

It had been almost as painful to see how much Jesus' friends grieved for Him—how much they loved Him. *They tried to comfort me,* she mused, *but you, Lord, gave me grace to comfort them instead. Now I understand why most of them fled. They were desperately afraid that Jesus' dream and vision died with Him.*

Mary's step quickened as she recalled what happened

next. Mary of Magdala was the first to find that empty tomb, and she had come running to tell everyone. It was true—Jesus lived! Mary warmed at the remembrance of seeing her son again, and she relived the magnificent joy she experienced when she and Jesus greeted each other. *He looked so majestic—healed, and beautiful,* Mary thought. At last the identity of her son would no longer remain a secret—at least not to those who had put their faith in Him before the Crucifixion.

For the next forty days, Jesus had lived among them again and had appeared to dozens of people, some of whom remained skeptical, Mary knew, until they touched His hands and side. And then, after eating with them and teaching them, Jesus had been taken up into the clear, blue air of a late-spring day, ascending to the Father.

As they walked, Mary and John spoke in hushed voices as they recalled the last thing Jesus had said before He left them: "You will receive power when the Holy Spirit comes on you, and you will be my witnesses in Jerusalem, and in all Judea and Samaria, and to the ends of the earth." At that moment, His reassuring presence had left little room for doubt.

But after His ascension, questions emerged: "How will we do what He has commanded us to do?" "What sort of power did He mean?" John and the others wondered aloud.

Peter was there already when they arrived at the temple courts. Mary basked in the unity and love among Jesus' followers. "Friends," Peter began . . . but his voice faltered. Starting slowly, then rising with a thunderous sound, a gust of wind swept through the courtyard. Stinging dust blew in their faces, and everyone had to shield his eyes. When the mysterious blast subsided, Mary looked up . . . and caught her breath in awe. What appeared to be flames were falling from the open sky. *Is something burning?* she wondered. From nowhere the flames fell, settling on the head of each one present. And then one of these strange, wondrous lightnings alighted upon Mary's forehead—and a joy flooded into her soul. She was barely aware of the buzz of animated talk that flooded the room, so taken up was she in wonder.

Peter and John tried to speak to each other, but to everyone's amazement, they were speaking new languages. A murmur of amazement rose from the surrounding crowd, as those gathered there from all different nations heard the news about Jesus spoken in a familiar language. Peter scanned the throng and overheard one man say, "These people are drunk. They've had too much wine."

At that, Peter drew himself up to his full height and commanded the crowd's attention. "These men are not drunk," he thundered, looking straight at the skeptic. "It's only nine o'clock in the morning!" And as the people quieted, Peter quoted from the prophet Joel.

Mary gazed at Peter in awe as he spoke. Understanding dawned in her heart, and she silently thanked God for sending His Holy Spirit just as He had promised. *There is something completely new about Peter,* she mused. He was speaking confidently, with authority and with compassion.

"Men of Israel, listen to this—Jesus of Nazareth was a man accredited by God to you by miracles, wonders, and signs, which God did among you through him, as you yourselves know," Peter announced. "This man was handed over to you by God's set purpose and foreknowledge. And you, with the help of wicked men, put Him to death by nailing Him to the cross. But God raised Him from the dead, freeing Him from the agony of death, because it was impossible for death to keep its hold on Him. . . . Therefore, let all Israel be assured of this—God has made this Jesus, whom you crucified, both Lord and Christ."

When Peter finished speaking, he explained how each person must respond: "Repent and be baptized . . . in the name of Jesus Christ, so that your sins may be forgiven. And you will receive the gift of the Holy Spirit. The promise is for you and your children and for all who are far off—for all whom the Lord our God will call."

Some turned angrily and walked away. But many, many more surged forward, crying out for repentance and baptism. John and the other disciples began organizing the crowd into small groups awaiting baptism. John walked in their midst, counting. "Three thousand," he said to Mary. "They all want to be baptized in the name of Jesus." Mary looked at him, both of them trying to take in the magnitude of this event. As John groped for words, Mary repeated a phrase she had recalled so many times throughout her life: "With God, nothing is impossible!"

Watching in wonder, Mary poured out her heart of gratitude and joy. *Lord, you have fulfilled once again what you promised. Now I see that your kingdom is forever. Peter is telling the truth, exactly as it happened. But it is you who enable Peter to speak with such presence and power. And it is you who draw all these people to yourself. My soul magnifies you, Lord!*

Empowered by God

Try as we may, we cannot fully imagine the impact those three days following the Crucifixion had on Mary.

Her son's body lay in a stone tomb just outside Jerusalem's walls. No mother's heart could know more grief than that of losing a son through such unjust, humiliating torture.

God allows us all to endure emotional valleys that shake the very foundations of our faith. When we walk through them, we may wonder at times whether God even remembers our name. We may cry out as Jesus did, "My God, my God, why have you forsaken me?" Yet in the darkest valley, a valley as foreboding as the one Mary walked, we can know that God cares. He did not abandon Mary in her grief, and most importantly, He saw her through to the other side. Knowing our sufferings, God watches and hurts with us. Psalm 56:8, says, "Thou hast taken account of my wanderings; put my tears in Thy bottle; are they not in Thy book? (KJV)" He doesn't miss a single tear. He knew every tear Mary shed while her son lay in the grave.

When Jesus cried out in despair, He was experiencing the depth of our sin. Sin cannot coexist with God, just as darkness cannot coexist with light. Jesus took upon himself the sin of all the world, dying to it literally so we could be reconciled to God. When we experience the weight of sin, either our own or someone else's, we sense the gulf that separates sinful men from God.

The story of Jesus does not end with sacrifice, with the Crucifixion. In fact, it has yet to end. After His suffering and death came the Resurrection. What unimaginable joy Mary must have felt! She had waited more than thirty-three years to see this fulfillment. Yet her suffering helped develop her character and increase her faith. God does not waste suffering. He uses it to forge character—if we yield it to Him. Suffering can make us *bitter* or *better*. The choice is ours.

The story is sometimes told of a woman who dreamed

that she saw the underside of a large tapestry. It was bright and colorful, yet she noted some very dark and snarled-looking sections of thread. She thought they looked out of place. Then the Lord told her the tapestry represented her life. She was amazed and said, "O Lord, it's so beautiful. If it weren't for those awful, colorless, dull and dark areas—those knots and frayed threads are distracting."

The Lord answered, "If only you could see your life's tapestry from *this* side. The design I am creating is more beautiful than you can see. The dark areas are necessary to its overall design, and the knotty places are where I tied it all together. It will be magnificent when I have finished!"

Our times of grief are part of God's grand design for our lives, and if we wait upon God they will lead to resurrection. When God is involved in our visions, hopes, and dreams, *nothing is impossible!*

Oswald Chambers, whose spiritual insights have blessed millions, encourages:

> When God gives a vision and darkness follows, *wait.* God will make you in accordance with the vision He has given if you will wait His time. Never try and help God fulfill His word.

At Pentecost, the disciples gained firsthand knowledge of this truth. They were not called to help God; rather, God was equipping them by sending the Holy Spirit to tell about Jesus. On that occasion, the presence of Mary and the other women with the disciples was significant. Jesus cut across social barriers, recognizing women as being *equal,* though not *identical* to men. This He did in a culture that held women so inferior that their testimony was not even considered valid in court. Women were judged unreliable. Even the first word of Jesus' resurrection, delivered by a woman, was met with disbelief from the male disciples.

Thetus Tenney speaks of this:

> Luke records an important detail concerning women in Acts 1:14: "These all continued with one accord in prayer and supplication with the women, and Mary the mother of Jesus and His brethren." Now the feast of Pentecost was traditionally celebrated only by Jewish males. But the fullness of time was approaching again. It was a time of spiritual change. The disciples did not know what to expect. Jesus had told them, "Go, tarry," but they did not fully understand. The men tarried—with the women! . . . It was an unusual thing for the women to be involved in spiritual matters.
>
> The Old Testament sign of the covenant, circumcision, totally excluded women. But with the changing of the times, water baptism became the sign of the new covenant. "For as many of you as have been baptized into Christ have put on Christ," Paul wrote to the Galatians. "There is neither Jew nor Greek, there is neither bond or free, there is neither male nor female: for ye all are in Christ Jesus" (Galatians 3:27, 28). We have all become sons, and as sons we share in the privileges; therefore we must also assume the responsibilities.[2]

Thus, Scripture attests to the equal importance of men *and* women in God's eyes. As Tenney asserts, God used many women to do the work of His church after Pentecost.

When we feel we are praying according to what we know about God's plan for our lives, or when He has called us to a particular vision or area of ministry, He also calls us to keep on praying and persevering. From beginning to end, what we learn of Mary in Scripture offers believers an example to follow no matter what their specific circumstances. She inclined herself toward prayer in good times and bad; she was accustomed to praising God and entreating Him. And perhaps one of her greatest gifts was that she knew how to wait for Him to answer, in His way, and in His own time.

On the day of Pentecost, Mary was with the disciples as they prayed in one accord. That united prayer produced an intimacy among those believers that human endeavor could not duplicate. As we look at her example, let us remember that Mary's last recorded act is prayer.

Questions to Ponder

1. Recall an emotional valley through which you had to walk. Did you sense God's presence there, or did you feel abandoned?
2. How could you incorporate the example of Mary's life into your approach to God, or your reaction to circumstances?
3. When you pray, do you take time to acknowledge the supreme sacrifice God made in our behalf? Take time today to thank Him for sending His only begotten Son, Jesus, who died for your sins.
4. Are you engaged in the work of the church, as Mary and the other women mentioned here were? What role can you play in fulfilling Jesus' Great Commission: "Therefore go and make disciples of all nations, baptizing them in the name of the Father and of the Son and of the Holy Spirit, and teaching them to obey everything that I commanded you. And surely I will be with you always, to the very end of the age" (Matthew 28:19, 20).

They devoted themselves to the apostles' teaching and to the
fellowship, to the breaking of bread and to prayer. Everyone
was filled with awe, and many wonders, and miraculous signs were
done by the apostles. All the believers were together and had
everthing in common. Selling their possessions and goods, they gave
to anyone as he had need. Every day they continued to meet
together in the temple courts. They broke bread in their homes and
ate together with glad and sincere hearts, praising God and enjoying
the favor of all the people. And the Lord added to their number daily
those who were being saved.

ACTS 2:42–47

But the fruit of the Spirit is love, joy, peace, patience, kindness,
goodness, faithfulness, gentleness and self-control. Against such
things there is no law. Those who belong to Christ Jesus have
crucified the sinful nature with its passions and desires. Since we live
by the Spirit, let us keep in step with the Spirit.

GALATIANS
5:22–25

12

A Model of True Womanhood

MARY REMAINED PRESENT with those first Christians, meeting and praying with them through the chaotic weeks following the Lord's resurrection and ascension. Together as one body of believers, the disciples found themselves empowered and equipped supernaturally to risk telling the good news of Jesus Christ.

The image of Mary among those disciples intrigues me and seems to suggest a lesson for today. Perhaps the earliest followers of Jesus drew strength and stability from Mary. Could she have served as a living reminder of the Lord's earthly existence—of the stunning truth that God took on human form in order to reach us and rescue us from sin? Might she have offered encouragement to other women who followed Jesus, modeling faith and obedience as well as active participation in the early church?

According to Scripture, Mary was not pushed aside by

those early Christians; she was welcomed among them. What about most of us today? In many cases, we pay scant attention to Mary. If we consider her at all, we frequently view her as a stumbling block; as a point of division in the Body of Christ.

It is my sincere prayer that Christians everywhere will come to see this extraordinary woman as a model, a steppingstone toward mutual respect and love among all believers. Is it really so outlandish to think that Mary, through what we know of her in the Bible, might serve as an example to men and women today?

The apostle Paul did not hesitate to tell his fellow Christians to look at him as an example. As I once heard a seminary student ask, "If we can find Jesus in other people, why can't we find him in Mary?" Virtuous character as portrayed in the life of this one woman is worthy of emulation—and virtue carries no expiration date. Today, all who follow Jesus can gain inspiration as we consider every role model available to us.

Kenneth Kantzer cites Mary as a model:

> What then, is the proper understanding about our relationship to the Virgin Mary? When we restrict ourselves to what is clearly taught in Scripture, we find in Mary a woman of beautiful character, uniquely blessed of God. She is an example of faith in God and a model for the church.
>
> Her faith held firm in spite of the extraordinary demands laid upon her. Unswerving faith in God, and the servant role she models for the whole church represent the essence of the biblical and evangelical view of Mary, the mother of Jesus.[1]

As we look to Mary as a model, our personal, individual walk with Christ can become richer. And as we look *together* at Mary, our witness as the Body of Christ will be challenged, too. On the night before He died, Jesus cried out to the Father, "that all of them may be one, Father, just as you are in me and I am in you. May they also be in us so that the world may believe that you sent me" (John 17:21).

Why is our oneness so important to Jesus? The unity of Spirit He described is a spiritual intimacy and great love among believers, and for all whom God created. When that is present in our worship and our ministries, then God is glorified. Love causes us to gather together, praising God and crying out for His will to be done. That kind of oneness with Him and with one another will change our hearts so that we long to do the things that please God: feeding the hungry, housing the homeless and clothing the naked (Isaiah 58). Imagine what that sort of oneness among Christians might bring—a living, breathing Body of Christ whose light would fill the earth, a church the world would not be able to overlook or ignore!

Consider this heartfelt plea from the apostle John: "Dear friends, since God so loved us, we also ought to love one another. No one has ever seen God; but if we love each other, God lives in us and his love is made complete in us" (1 John 4:11–12).

Is there a practical way that the Body of Christ, the Church, can achieve a functional oneness, when we see so many differences among us? If it is to happen, the Holy Spirit must knit us together, even as He knit together the followers of Jesus on the day of Pentecost. He can do this when we gather together at Jesus' feet, focusing only on Him in praise and worship. Doing this may not be easy. It may involve setting aside differences that are marginal to the real issue of salvation through Christ. It will mean reconsidering our personal judgments of others and their errors. It may mean humbly releasing to Jesus our long-standing traditions. As we learn to open our hearts to the Holy Spirit's softening and correction, it helps to recall that we simply cannot know all of God's plan and purpose while we remain on earth. In truth, all of us "see but a poor reflection" (1 Corinthians 13:12).

Protestants do not accept many of the Marian doctrines or devotions of the Catholic church. In urging Protestants to take another look at Mary, I do not suggest that they embrace beliefs and practices they cannot accept. Nonetheless, I believe genuine doctrinal differences do not rule out our need for compassion, understanding, and bridge-building for the sake of the whole kingdom of God. Arriving at a proper appreciation of Mary can help move us in that direction.

Mary's life, properly viewed, always points to Jesus, and He is the only one who can draw us together by His Holy Spirit. As His prayer for oneness among believers becomes our priority—and becomes our prayer as well—it may help us to grow in our knowledge and appreciation of His mother. We might begin by finding some common points of agreement about the things she said and did. Remember, the last quoted words of Mary that we find in the Bible were directed toward the servants at Cana: "Do whatever He tells you." Her wise and practical instructions to the servants speak just as clearly today, to all who claim Jesus as their Lord and Savior.

Finding Our Worth in Christ

Mary's universal traits cause the story of her life to address us all—and of course it is to women that she offers the most eloquent example. Mary's radical faith saw her through challenges, trials, and joys to which we women and mothers today can only wonder. Because of her faithfulness and willing obedience to God, Mary persevered through much: a miraculous conception; giving birth under perilous circumstances; hearing a sobering prophecy about her son; fleeing to Egypt for His safety; searching for Him in Jerusalem; seeing Him mature; watching in horror as he was arrested, tortured, and killed; and finally, taking her place among the Lord's other disciples and followers.

I believe that understanding and appreciating Mary can be a master-key to unlocking God's plan for women. *Mary knew who she was,* and she modeled womanhood in a magnificent manner. And yet she was one of us. The scholar, Leonard Foley, explains what this means for us today:

> Mary is not a woman protected from the demands of faith in daily living. There is nothing vapid or sentimental about her. She is a woman with her feet planted firmly on the earth—Mary of Nazareth, the new Eve, the new Mother of all the living, the woman whose risk in faith first made Christ present among us.
>
> It is precisely in this way that Mary is the first model for the contemporary woman—not as a mysterious icon or an object of obscure veneration and unattainable blessedness, but as an altogether human woman who was painfully misunderstood by the man she loved; who was confused by her child's behavior; who was not afraid to speak her mind or voice her questions; who stood by courageously while her son was executed; who was present at the outpouring of the Holy Spirit on the new Church; and who, indeed, had a role of leadership in that Church. . . .
>
> When Mary's place in the life and continued ministry of the Church is recognized and understood, the

place of all women in the Church is assured—not as onlookers or maidservants, but as integral co-workers, as necessary for the incarnation of Christ in our world as Mary was to the first Incarnation.[2]

Many women might ask, "What can I do? I'm so busy caring for my family; I have young children and can't get involved outside my home." A woman who remains at home can be as much a part of the spiritual battle as those who are involved outside their homes to influence the world for God.

The truth is, none of us can find our full identity in any*one* or any*thing*—only in the God who made us. That is a primary lesson of healthy spirituality. If you look to your spouse for your identity you will be disappointed, for we all fail at one time or another. No person can give you what only God has for you—a sense of personhood that withstands all circumstances.

And if you expect the world to tell you who you are, you will also be disappointed. The world doesn't know or care who you are, unless you have wealth, celebrity, power, or title. All of these, however, are transitory, and beyond them, the world generally has no interest in you or me. But if we rest our identity in the God who made us, who calls each of us by name, then the way you talk and walk, act and live will tell the world *whose* you are. The people around you will know that you belong to Jesus!

Second, hold on to the common aspects of Mary's example, and remember what she was doing when God called her: going about the mundane chores of her everyday life—when eternity interrupted. In the same way, most of us are called to remain faithful in the little things of life. As God sees us faithfully carry out our obligations to home, family, and community, He will strengthen our obedience. And He will give us unmistakable opportunities to involve ourselves in work of eternal significance.

As we have seen, God slowly prepared Mary for His greater work in her life, drawing on her established habits of humble obedience. That sort of steadfast growth leads to godly confidence, and helps us to say yes to God, even if His direction is vastly different from what we expect.

Mary also gives us the light of *purity* and *courage*. The amazing announcement of her pregnancy by the Holy Spirit, coming before her marriage to Joseph, might have been cause for despair or self-pity. Yet, Mary rejoiced in what God was doing in her life. Remaining obedient to God mattered more to her than the opinions of people who may have assumed she'd been unfaithful to Joseph. Her eternal perspective regarding what was happening in her life offers us an eloquent example of remaining steadfast, unmoved by the shifting currents of contemporary life.

How did Mary cope with what we might call a crisis pregnancy? Again, her actions speak convincingly to us today. Mary sought the companionship of her older cousin, Elizabeth, who after many years of barrenness was expecting her own miracle baby. Mary took the initiative to share her joy and her questions, and together the two women praised God and encouraged each other's faith. What a remarkably relevant picture they present for us today! Imagine what our Christian community would be like if believers consistently sought one another out to share hurts and hopes, dreams, and doubts—in the light of Christ's work in their lives.

In her Magnificat—her song of praise—Mary modeled praise and worship for us as well as familiarity with God's Word. When His Word is our daily companion, then praising God with the very psalms and songs of Holy Scripture comes naturally. Cultivating a spirit of praise, and a comfortable knowledge of Scripture are two ways we can respond to God and open ourselves to the leading of His still small voice.

Along with Joseph, Mary remained faithful in observing the requirements of her Jewish faith. She participated in the Passover observance and performed the required rituals following childbirth. Just because God touched her life in an extraordinary way, Mary did not consider herself above other people. She did not exhibit any spiritual pride, but remained obedient to God and to her husband. Our faithful observance of worship, Bible study, prayer, and other practices of our faith are important for each of us, no matter how far we've progressed along the road to spiritual maturity. If Mary continued to express humble thanks and worship to God through established channels, how much more should we?

Mary also models *self-control*. Remember, she was a ponderer, hiding the things God revealed to her in her heart. This is a counterbalance to the trait of seeking fellowship and sharing our thoughts with other believers. Both are important; they do not cancel one another out. We need to pray for godly wisdom to know when God should be our only confidant, and when we should share our heart with a trusted friend.

At Cana, Mary is portrayed as being *observant* and *empathetic*. She apparently was the first to observe that the wine had run out, threatening to spoil the wedding feast. She draws the situation to Jesus' attention without ordering Him around. The larger spiritual significance of this event, of course, involves Jesus performing His first miracle: turning water into wine. As we have seen, it was Mary who recognized that His time had come. Are we observant about the situations around us? Is there someone we know who is lacking something we might provide? Would we call God's attention to a dilemma in the same way Mary did—without telling Him exactly what He should do?

As a mother, Mary challenges us to *relinquish* our children to God's purposes. Beginning perhaps at the temple in Jerusalem, Mary had to acknowledge Jesus' unique call. She had to let Him go, and yet continue to serve as His mother. Their relationship began changing then, and kept on changing until Mary herself became one of the Lord's disciples, meeting and praying with the young church. When we sense that our relationship with a child is changing, it may be difficult to accommodate that change; we may be tempted to live in the past or to try to conform our child's life to our expectations. Letting go is not easy, but Mary helps show us how.

Within her larger family, Mary emerges in Scripture as a *peacemaker*. When certain relatives of Jesus wanted to take Him away from the crowds, believing He was out of His mind, Mary took the initiative to go directly to Him and attempt to set things straight. She displays a spirit of honesty and a commitment to maintaining and repairing hurt relationships. This may present one of the most difficult challenges of all, yet I believe women are uniquely equipped by God to serve in this way. And how much better off our families will be when we actively seek to preserve peace and harmony at home!

Nor did Mary's devotion to Jesus fail her even at His darkest hour. As she stood by Him throughout the agony of the Crucifixion and the preparations for burial, Mary exhibits unflagging love and dedication to her son and Lord. She knew all along that a sword would pierce her own soul, and still she persevered as a parent. Raising children today may be the biggest personal commitment we make, and most parents go into it knowing serious challenges may await them. A child may face physical, emotional, or spiritual trials in which we cannot intervene, except through prayer and our tenacious presence as loving mothers and fathers.

Finally, Mary goes on to offer a pattern for older women whose children are grown and whose main work in life appears finished. After Jesus' ascension, Mary stayed active with the church, seeing it through the dangers of its infancy. So, too, can we remain involved as we grow older. Being faithful to God's call does not come with a time limit; a life habit of obedience to Him is one we should cultivate and maintain, just as Mary did.

Coming to Full Bloom

When God created woman, He gave her certain gifts and sensitivities in a greater measure than He gave to most men, as part of the nurturing gifts needed in mothering. Women are not only the mothers of humankind—they are the heart of humankind. Just as the heart performs a crucial bodily function, a woman's function in her family, in the Body of Christ, and in the world is crucial.

Often, we find it difficult to comprehend that God is above gender, for we live in a world naturally divided between male and female. Yet God's nature supersedes gender. I believe Mary models Jesus for the female gender. She reflects the sweet fragrance of Christ's character as she exhibits the fruit of the Spirit—love, joy, peace, longsuffering, kindness, goodness, faithfulness, gentleness, self-control (Galatians 5:22, 23).

And how we need that fruit in our lives today, at a

time when women find themselves under attack in so many ways! In a *Washington Post* article, Lori Heise wrote, "Violence against women—including assault, mutilation, murder, infanticide, rape, and cruel neglect—is perhaps the most pervasive yet least recognized human-rights issue in the world. . . ." She cited particular instances of violence against women around the world and concluded, "In all these instances, women are targets of violence because of their sex. This is not random violence. The risk factor is being female."[3]

As I observe what is happening today, particularly in America, I must conclude with sorrow that our pain is sometimes self-inflicted. Beginning in the 1950s and 1960s, women started battling ideologies and policies they felt were oppressive. Many changes have come about because of the women's movement. Some have been good. Some have brought only more distortion and confusion. Some women denied their womanhood; some started seeing marriage as a form of bondage, and men as the enemy; some denigrated motherhood and the home; some fell victim to the same sins they resented in men; some sought their identity in careers.

In today's America, we see women stripped of virtue and dignity in various ways. The so-called sexual revolution invited exploitation, which now pervades television programming, movies, and advertisements. Appallingly, some women not only tolerate, but actually participate in this debasement. As the prodigal son saw himself in the pigpen, realizing that he was too good for his present condition, we women need to see ourselves and realize the high call God has placed on our lives.

God wants us to fully realize our worth and value in Him. Women, as all human beings, have intrinsic value in the Lord's eyes. They also have tremendous value to society. Some historians through the years have noted the great worth of women in society. The French historian, Alexis de Tocqueville, wrote in his work *Democracy in America,* "If anyone asks me what I think the chief cause of the extraordinary prosperity and growing power of this nation, I should answer that it is due to the superiority of her women."[4]

De Tocqueville wrote this in the early 1800s, before women were permitted to vote in America! Yet he correctly perceived women as the source of powerful influence that positively affected society. Women have often brought about change by being a conscience long-denied. And history teaches us that the courageous and selfless leadership of a few can change the course of many. Through history, the influence of women has played a decisive role. President Abraham Lincoln cited Harriet Beecher Stowe's novel *Uncle Tom's Cabin* as the chief cause of changing public opinion about slavery. Yet, women have not always understood their importance, nor have many men understood and appreciated the vital role women play in our culture.

Perhaps Mary's model of womanhood could remind us that true femininity never becomes outdated. The Holy Spirit's power at work in the lives of godly women is not weakened or compromised by feminine behavior, dress, or manner of speech. Perhaps we need to see ourselves as feminine rather than feminist, and let our bearing command the dignity and respect women deserve. Perhaps then we will see the restoration of true femininity.

Women must exercise their influence, not just in earthly matters but in the spiritual realm as well. We have great influence with our Father in heaven through prayer, and great influence for our Father as we seek to follow His lead in our lives.

Women were created to be responders. This doesn't imply that women never initiate anything—it's just an observation about the general makeup of women. Women respond to love, to needs, and to others. They also are sensitive to and respond more easily to God's call. In addition, women were created to be receivers. Mary responded when Gabriel announced God's plan to her, and received in her womb by the Holy Spirit the seed which produced Jesus. Today, women can respond and receive the spiritual seeds God wants to plant in their hearts.

Orthodox scholar Mary Ann De Trana offers these words of wisdom for women and men wrestling over the question of women's liberation. As she cites Mary's example, De Trana points out one of the paradoxes of the kingdom: True freedom is to be in the captivity of the Liberator.

> True freedom can only be realized in submitting ourselves, our bodies, our minds, our wills, all of our talents and possessions to do God's will. . . . Truly the only real freedom is complete and absolute submission to God's will, as [Mary] did.[5]

Woman has been like a rosebud set in a vase. A rosebud is lovely and its fragrance is sweet, yet restrained. As any flower-lover knows, a rosebud should not be forced into bloom by pulling its petals open. If forced, the flower loses its beauty, fragrance, and potential for full bloom. It will wither and die before its time.

The world and the enemy have tried to restrain women from their full potential. Some women have even sought counterfeit ways to come to full bloom. Both attempts have denied or distorted womanhood as the Master Gardener intended. Only the Creator God can call forth that bloom, as women submit to Him in faith and obedience.

The sweet fragrance of woman in the fullness of bloom will please her Creator and attract the people around her. In 2 Corinthians 2:15 we learn that "we are to God the aroma of Christ among those who are being saved and those who are perishing."

And many are perishing. The world is hungry for the "Bread of Life"—hungry to meet the Savior it so desperately needs, but woefully ignorant of the object of its unfulfilled desire. And everyone, man or woman, who calls himself by Christ's name is mandated to take the Gospel to all the world. Yet here is that special thought for women: When God was ready to move on the earth—to send His Son—He first told a woman. And through faith, she moved in obedience. She yielded herself to His perfect will, and God accomplished His purposes.

Bearing Light and Peace

There is a Jewish ceremony that accompanies the arrival of the Sabbath on Fridays at sundown. To me, it symbolizes what Mary was called to do 2,000 years ago and what women are called to do today. The ceremony is explained in the book by Rabbi Hayim Halevy Donin, *To Be a Jew*:

> Lighting of the Sabbath candles formally ushers in the Sabbath for the members of the household.
>
> It is the obligation of the wife to fulfill this religious duty. . . .
>
> The Sabbath candles are lighted approximately twenty minutes before sundown. . . . Once the time of sundown passes, the candles may no longer be lit. . . .
>
> The blessing recited for the Sabbath candles is:
> Blessed art Thou, Lord our God, King of the uni-

verse, who has sanctified us with His commandments and commanded us to kindle the Sabbath lights.

After the candles are lit, it is proper to greet the others in the household with the words Shabbat Shalom (Sabbath Peace). Everyone responds likewise. . . . [6]

In this ceremony the Jewish woman brings the light. She must light the candle at the proper time, just before the Sabbath begins at sundown. In the same way, God sent His son, born of a woman in the proper time. Mary, the Jewish woman Jesus called mother, brought forth the light of the world!

The time I have spent learning about Mary has enriched my own personal walk with the Lord immeasurably. In Mary, I see the sort of woman God is calling me to be. I believe this can be true for every woman who has committed her life to Jesus. The many facets of Mary's faith illuminate the ways in which belief may be put into practice, whatever our circumstances may be. And, most importantly, Mary directs my attention inevitably toward her son. My prayer is that this book will encourage the kind of appreciation of Mary that leads to complete devotion to Jesus. "All generations will call me blessed," Mary prophesied. This generation, as it seeks to respond to God in faith and obedience, should be no exception.

The Song of Solomon asks, "Who is this coming up out of the wilderness leaning on her Beloved?" (Song of Solomon 8:5). I long for the day when the world will look around in surprise and echo that verse, asking, "Who is this coming up out of the wilderness leaning on her Beloved?" They will see God's Church coming up, bearing the Lord's light and peace—not with striving and turmoil, but humbly and obediently, yet in great strength, brought forth by our beloved Lord Jesus Christ!

Acknowledgments

There are so many to whom I would like to give thanks for their assistance in the writing of this book. It was difficult for me to write, and it was only by the grace of God that it is finally completed, I thank Him.

I thank Ruth Reitz Ford, my first and able editor, who helped pull a long and diverse manuscript that had been sitting on the shelf into better order. I also thank the editors from Bethany house, who labored on the final version of *Jesus Called Her Mother*. Then, of course, there were innumerable researchers, theologians, historians, and others whose works I reviewed during the writing of this book. Last, but certainly not least, I thank my husband, Roger, who supported and encouraged me over the three years of writing, thinking, and talking about it, as I wrestled time from a busy schedule of travel to work on "the Mary book." It's finally done! My prayer is that is pleased with all our efforts.

Dee Jepsen

Notes

Chapter 1

1. Charles Spurgeon, *Morning and Evening* (Grand Rapids: Zondervan Publishing House, 1980).
2. Richard N. Ostling, "The Search for Mary," *Time*, Dec. 30, 1991, p. 62.
3. Kenneth S. Kantzer, "A Most Misunderstood Woman," *Christianity Today*, Dec. 12, 1986, p. 20.
4. Luci Shaw, "Yes to Shame and Glory," *Christianity Today*, Dec. 12, 1986, p. 22.

Chapter 2

1. Alfred Edersheim, *Sketches of Jewish Social Life in the Days of Christ*. (Grand Rapids, Mich.: Wm. B. Eerdmans Publishing Co., 1985), p. 36.
2. Ibid., pp. 148, 155.
3. Leviticus 20:10; John 8:5.
4. Jamie Buckingham, *A Way Through the Wilderness* (Chosen Books, 1983).
5. George Sweeting, "A Mother Chosen By God," *Moody Monthly*, Vol. 82, No. 9, May 1982, p. 21.
6. *Strong's Exhaustive Concordance* #2428.

Chapter 3

1. Alfred Edersheim, *Sketches in Jewish Social Life in the Days of Christ*, pp. 132, 133.
2. *Ibid.,* p. 36.
3. Raymond E. Brown, *et. al.*, editors, *Mary in the New Testament* (Philadelphia: Fortress Press, 1978), pp. 132, 133.
4. A. Moody Stuart, *The Three Marys* (Edinburgh, Scotland: *The Banner of Truth*, 1984), pp. 228–229.
5. Raymond E. Brown, *et. al.*, editors, *Mary in the New Testament*, p. 142.

Chapter 4

1. John F. MacArthur, *The MacArthur New Testament Commentary* (Chicago: Moody Press, 1986), pp. 17, 18.
2. Frederick Buechner, "And Nothing was the Same Again," *The Lutheran*, Dec. 14, 1988, p. 6.

Chapter 5

1. Madeleine S. Miller and J. Lane Miller, *Harper's Encyclopedia of Bible Life* (San Francisco: Harper & Row, 1978), p. 97.
2. Jean Guitton, *The Virgin Mary* (New York: P. J. Kenedy & Sons, 1949), p. 39.
3. John F. MacArthur, *MacArthur New Testament Commentary,* pp. xi, xii, 2, 3.

Chapter 6

1. John F. MacArthur, *MacArthur New Testament Commentary*, p. 26

Chapter 7

1. D. Guthrie, *et. al.*, editors, *The New Bible Commentary*, revised ed. (Grand Rapids: Wm. B. Eerdmans Publishing Co., 1970).
2. Paul J. Achtemeier, General Editor, *Harper's Bible Dictionary*, (San

Francisco: Harper & Row, 1985) p. 754.
3. Alfred Edersheim, *Sketches of Jewish Life in the Days of Christ.*

Chapter 8

1. Basilea Schlink, *Mary, the Mother of Jesus* (Marshall Pickering, Basingstoke, England, 1986).
2. Luci Shaw, "Yes to Shame and Glory," *Christianity Today*, Dec. 12, 1986, p. 24.
3. Fulton J. Sheen, *The World's First Love* (Garden City, N.Y.: Image Books, 1952), p. 138.
4. *The Complete Biblical Library* (Springfield: Gospel Publishing House, 1991), p. 51.
5. Fulton J. Sheen, p. 139.

Chapter 9

1. C. Milo Connick, *Jesus, the Man and the Message* (Englewood Cliffs, N.J.: Prentice Hall, Inc., 1963), pp. 178, 179.
2. Fulton J. Sheen, *The World's First Love*, pp. 124, 125.

Chapter 10

1. C. Milo Connick, p. 386.

Chapter 11

1. Luci Shaw, p. 24.
2. Thetus Tenney, "God Sent Forth . . . Made of a Woman," *Focused Light* p. 101.

Chapter 12

1. Kenneth Kantzer, p. 21.
2. Leonard Foley, O.F.M., "Mary: Woman Among Us," *Catholic Update*, 1987, p. 2.

3. Lori Heise, "The Global War Against Women," *The Washington Post,* April 9, 1989, p. B–1.
4. Alexis de Tocqueville, *Democracy in America.*
5. Mary Ann De Trana, *Mary, Model for the Church and So for All of Us* (Unpublished paper), pp. 30, 31.
6. Hayim Haleyy Donin, *To Be a Jew* (New York: Basic Books, Inc.,), pp. 72, 73.